❧ TABLE OF CONTENTS ❧

Jeffrey A. Gall

～ INTRODUCTION: ～
WHY FAMILY ON MISSION?

Have you ever listened to a young child learning to play an instrument? It is an exercise in patience and endurance! Of course it is, because the child is learning to do something she doesn't know how to do yet. What's interesting, though, is that the thing about music that's easiest to learn is the *structure*—which notes to play, how long to play them, when to rest. What's more difficult is learning the *texture* of music—the dynamics of playing loudly or softly, using a crescendo or decrescendo, finding the right tone and pace. The structure often comes first, but even when a song is technically played correctly, it can still be a long way off from an enjoyable piece of music. The *texture* is what makes the *structure* work as a piece of art.

Structure without texture just doesn't work, on a number of levels. Think about the human body. The skeletal structure is absolutely key to making the body work, but nobody wants to be hugged by a skeleton. Just imagine the awkward angularity of two skeletons trying to hug, or shake hands, or do anything human, really. We need the texture of muscle, ligament, tendon, and skin if we are to interact as humans. Structure without texture doesn't work. Structure and texture are intended to work together.

It's the same in our pursuit of discipleship and mission. Over the years we have trained a lot of leaders in missional discipleship, and as we've done so we started noticing something interesting happening. People often put the structure of discipleship and mission into place, but then come back to us scratching their heads, because it doesn't seem to be working. In other words, structure alone doesn't produce the kinds of results they expected. The framework of discipleship failed to deliver the functionality of a family on mission.

What we began to realize is that they had been implementing the *structure* of discipleship, but weren't catching the *texture* of the process that truly mobilizes and empowers people to be on mission. They taught the structure but needed training in the texture of discipleship and mission. They were technically correct, playing all the right notes at the right time, but needed to grow into the dynamic of the music in order to masterfully play the song!

So we began reflecting on what the *texture* of our disciple-making process was. What did we see Jesus doing in the Gospels that we were imitating and implementing in our own disciple-making? We began talking about it as a couple and with our team here at 3DM, and we started asking questions about the way we had been doing things, and how we learned to do them. Those conversations were where this book began.

What we are calling **family on mission** is the *texture* of discipleship that allows the *structure* to do its job. Family on mission is the music to the lyrics of discipleship. Family on mission is how we stop thinking of discipleship as a *task* that we *do* and start living out discipleship as a way that we *are*. Family on mission is how we stop doing discipleship as a class, program, or curriculum, and start living it as a way of life.

Here's the bottom line: discipleship and mission never really work unless we are able to create the *texture* of **family on mission**. Without the "soft tissue" of a family on mission, this discipleship stuff will be just another program we'll forget about in a few months, and mission will be just another activity we need to fit into our already busy schedule. If we're going to make disciples and move out in mission, we need to go from managing boundaries between the compartments of our lives to integrating family and mission into **one life**, a cohesive framework and fabric that empowers a *culture* of discipleship and mission, not just occasional events and periodic programs.

We need to learn how to live out the texture as we implement the structure. That's what this book is intended to help you move toward.

We (Mike and Sally) have written this book together, along with help from the Content Team at 3DM. If you've ever seen us together at an event or webinar, you'll likely recognize in this book the way we function when we speak together. Sally typically tells stories about how it all looked in real life (even if it isn't very flattering), and Mike typically reflects on the theological structure behind it all. In other words, Mike brings the structure, but Sally brings the texture that makes the structure work. You'll know very quickly why we wanted to write this book together when you read Sally's account of our journey into family on mission in the first chapter.

The two voices are marked in the text with an indication of who is writing at the beginning of each section, as well as with a different background behind each voice. Mike has bricks behind his voice (for structure), and Sally has swirly designs behind her voice (for texture).

So imagine yourself sitting down with us in our living room, near the fireplace with a nice cup of tea (we're English, after all), so we can simply have a long conversation about the structure and texture of being a **family on mission**.

1

~ OUR JOURNEY TO ~ FAMILY ON MISSION

DON'T EVER, EVER DATE THIS GUY

Sally Writes:

I was sixteen. He entered through the door of our battered, smelly youth hall in suburban Manchester late one Saturday evening during the long, hot summer of 1974. He left his bike outside but brought his smile and long legs inside. I welcomed him and introduced him to another guy around his age: my boyfriend. We all became good friends and hung around as a group all summer, playing Pink Floyd records, drinking coffee, and talking passionately about how to reach and disciple the lost and the lonely. Oftentimes, late at night after work or youth group, he stopped on his walk home to feed the homeless and offer them hope. We would sit for hours and talk theology.

Mike ended up leading us that summer, and shaping us. In particular, he ended up shaping me. I was a hippie, barefoot, flowers-in-the-hair kind of girl. Lots of smiling, not much studying. Lots of laughter and singing, not much natural discipline. But a heart wide open for evangelism. The summer we met we were young, passionate, and stupid. In one of the many conversations that went deep into the evening, I asked him a question, as we sat on the floor with a Beatles song playing in the background. It was a common question any sixteen-year-old would ask: "What are you going to be when you grow up?"

> **I WAS A HIPPIE, barefoot, flowers-in-the-hair kind of girl.**

He didn't give it a second thought, didn't even pause for breath. "I'm going to be a missionary," he said. Immediately two thoughts collided in my scattered brain. First: **don't ever, ever date this guy!** He is the kind who would drag you to foreign lands, carrying a large heavy black Bible, wearing unfashionable clothes. And second: **he's really serious about this.** He was going "all in" for God! The most obvious track to take for someone like that at the time was to become an ordained minister in the Church of England, and this was the track Mike was on.

Despite my vow to never date this guy, somewhere along the way, between the movies, the bike rides and the intense conversations, I forgot about it and did actually date him. Not only did I date him, but I also eventually married him. On an early rainy September morning in 1980, in front of our family and friends, in the church where we met, we began our life together. I was twenty-two years old, standing at the edge of an adventure.

FAMILY OR MISSION

We started out living in an apartment in a place called Hackney, the worst public housing estate in the United Kingdom. We had no money, no car, no furniture, no friends, and definitely no cell phones. We didn't even have a working pay phone nearby.

As we began this new season of ordained ministry, we talked a lot about what we saw in other pastors' families. Many of them were simply a disaster. It was obvious they had put the church ahead of their families. Their children were frequently rebellious or alienated; the wives were sad, depressed or simply angry. There was lots of difficulty and dysfunction in their homes.

> WE TALKED A LOT **about what we saw in other pastors' families. So many of them were simply a disaster.**

I had seen this up close when Mike was in seminary. Every Sunday he was assigned to visit a different church, and many times I went with him. After the morning service, we would have lunch at the pastor's house, and the lunch would be a *completely* different environment from the church service in the morning. More often than not, we ate lunch in a dull, depressing house with chaotic children and an overwhelmed wife who was trying to keep it all together. It was such a stark contrast to the beautiful, carefully presented worship service in the church. I had a deep sympathy for these people.

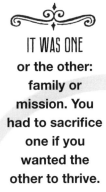

I knew I didn't want our lives to be like that, and neither did Mike. We didn't want Mike to run to his church work to avoid the people and problems in his own family. I didn't want to end up bitter and angry, or cold and passionless. But it seemed inevitable! This is how it seemed to work. You could have **family *or* mission, but they didn't seem to work very well together**.

Many of the people who led great ministries that brought revival and transformation to the church left their children behind so they could go to the mission field. Many spent very little time with their children or spouse, devoting most of their time to preaching sermons and writing books. It probably seemed heroic at the time, and God worked through their lives, but generally it was a disaster for the families. No one had ever trained these leaders to lead a ministry and lead a family. It was assumed they would just work it out. But it wasn't working.

It seemed like it was always one or the other; you could have a great ministry, or you could have a great family, but you couldn't have both. It was one or the other: **family *or* mission**. You had to sacrifice one if you wanted the other to thrive. And since being a pastor seemed like a godly calling, maybe having a terrible family life was just part of the package. Others we saw chose family over mission. They would abandon all their dreams of wider mission and ministry so they could have a functional family.

We desperately wanted to find out if there was another option.

FAMILY AND MISSION

So we talked about this in the car on long journeys, over dinner, and at the kitchen sink while drying dishes. I kept coming back to this overwhelming sense that we needed to be "normal," which meant that I wanted us to be able to look, sound, and behave normally, without abandoning God's call on our lives. We weren't going to project some weird, fake version of ourselves; we were going to be normal.

We were going to try and do **family _and_ mission**. We were not going to let mission make our family life miserable. We resolved somehow to find a way to do these two callings at the same time, running on parallel tracks, moving in the same direction. We would work out ways of building our life so it had good boundaries and plenty of margin. Our goal was to have a great family _and_ a great ministry.

While we were newlyweds living in Hackney, I took a job as a realtor in London. Mike was an inner-city youth worker studying for his master's degree in theology. I worked 9 AM to 5 PM and he worked 4 PM to midnight with the youth. When he got home at midnight, he stayed up until 2 AM studying and writing papers. Every day, we met for lunch in an old bakery and caught up with each other over tea and toast. I dragged an old beanbag into the study so I could sleep there to the steady tapping of the typewriter rather than be alone. It was challenging, but it worked. We juggled and stretched and made it work.

When I was in college, I was voted "Girl Least Likely to Ever Have Children." However, on the bright, sunny morning of June 6, 1984, overlooking the cornfields of the Cambridge countryside, I gave birth to our beautiful daughter Rebecca Jane. I loved her deeply. I completely and utterly loved being a mom. It took me by surprise, actually. I used to call my mom and tell her, in amazement, "I still like her!" and "I still like me, too!" Such a gift, a child. A child to take care of, to nurture, to disciple and to discipline. Raising a child is a complicated and confusing experience and takes us to the cross quicker and more often than any other process I know. But of course we were going to do family _and_ mission, so alongside this new role of being a mom and building a family, I still loved mission and all that meant for us in this season.

OUR GOAL
was to have a great family and a great ministry.

By now, we had moved to Cambridge and Mike was in charge of youth ministry across the city. I still had a big heart for the lost and the lonely. It was just a bit more complicated to carry it out as I moved slowly carrying a six-month-old on my hip or pushing a stroller. But we were OK with that—we would simply add boundaries and margins and plan more! We were capable, intelligent people; we should be able to do both areas of our lives, family and mission, and do them well. We had our mission life, and we had our family life. We wanted both to be great, and we worked toward both being great.

WE HAD CLEAR **boundaries between ministerial life and family life.**

We had clear boundaries between ministerial life and family life, and we needed to manage those boundaries and make sure we had enough margin within those boundaries when things got difficult. We knew there would be times when things wouldn't function perfectly and ministry life could extend over into family life, so we needed to build in margin. That way, even in times of stress, it wouldn't threaten our life or our ministry.

We had our mission life and our family life, and like pouring water into different containers, we managed the energy we put into each reality, attempting to move our family and our mission toward health and fruitfulness. We measured and poured our time and energy into each container, watching it closely, checking it against the other. Always asking questions: "Which one is getting more? Which one is suffering?" It was not OK for either one to fail. We developed clear boundaries, putting in rhythms, taking days off, going on vacations, managing the stress, managing the vision, and managing time all the time.

We functioned this way for about ten years. They were good years, but not great years, if I'm honest. Not particularly fulfilling to either of us. Our worlds were very often separate. We now had four children (three biological and one adopted teenage foster daughter), a new church, a large rundown house and a larger vision. During those ten years I went from carefree, passionate hippie to lawgiver and accountant. I watched the clock. I watched Mike. I watched if he was ten minutes late coming home for supper. I watched the amount of time he spent out in the evenings at meetings. I counted how many Saturdays he took the children swimming. I asked, "When is it going to be my turn to do something exciting? When do I get a day off?"

Don't get me wrong—I loved raising the children. They brought me an immense amount of fulfillment and joy, but there were sometimes moments when I sat alone on the sofa, wondering whether Mike was running ahead of me spiritually, and whether I would ever catch up. On many occasions, I was simply too tired to really care about the "new strategy for mission" that Mike was talking about. And Mike was often too distracted to really hear me talk about my successes of the day: wiping noses, changing diapers, and separating arguing children.

So we were doing **family *and* mission**, looking confident and competent, not sacrificing one for the other, accomplishing both. It was fine for a while, not an absolute disaster or anything, and far better than doing **family OR mission**. But we were discovering that **family AND mission** is an utterly exhausting way to function. Trying to keep everything in its own container, managing the boundaries between ministry and family all the time, had become unsustainable for us.

And it wasn't that we were bad at it! We were actually pretty good at managing the boundaries. You get proficient at it after ten years. But it was so, so tiring. We found that we were expending so much energy managing boundaries that we weren't able to do other important things, like **making disciples**, which was the call we had both received at the beginning of our adventure together!

We had just finished a call to an inner-city church in the poorest community in England, a place called Brixton Hill, and what's interesting is that we did a lot of great, innovative ministry there. But today, there's hardly anything left, no evidence of an ongoing work of God that continued after we left.[1] The reason was that we were managing our ministry well, but we weren't making disciples who were making disciples. We were beginning to realize that **you can't make disciples if you're constantly managing boundaries.**

We looked at all of it and thought, "There has to be a better way to do this."

FAMILY ON MISSION

So we continued to talk and talk and talk, this time interrupted by the cries and chatter of little ones, disturbed by pressing phone calls and meetings. But

---

[1] You can read more about this story, and how we changed things when we moved to Sheffield, in our book *Leading Kingdom Movements*.

somewhere between teatime and team meetings, we began to wonder, "What would happen if we invited more people into our lives?" Not inviting more people over to entertain them, but simply inviting them into what we were already doing to help us. At first it did seem a little counter-intuitive to invite *more* people into our already busy lives. We were already hard-pressed— wouldn't that create more stress?

But we had a hunch that it might just be the answer. So we tried it. We began inviting people into everything, into the mealtimes and into the mission. We included more people in our life, to help us in the little things and the big things, in our family and in our mission. We found some poor, unsuspecting young adults who were on the outer edges of our life, and said to them, "Come walk with us." We just included them when grocery shopping and folding laundry and praying for the sick. We asked them to babysit our kids, help them with their homework, do administrative tasks, run youth events. Much to our amazement, what we found was that none of them were put off by the small, loud children who came as part of the package. They actually loved the normality and the noise of it all.

Some of the simple things of family life brought real joy to single men and women who were becoming part of the fabric of our lives, things like reading bedtime stories to the kids while I cleaned up supper to get ready for an evening meeting. Some of them gained healing and hope along the way. Some of them had real talent in different areas, and callings to lead. We had no money to pay them properly, so they just lived with us. It seemed that when we moved as a group, we were actually more effective in our family stuff *and* our mission! To top it all off, because people were now coming along with us in our normal everyday lives, we had ample time to actually disciple them.

Our previously neatly defined boundaries between family life and mission life began to blur like heavy rain on a windshield. We forgot to manage margins, and our boundaries were technically "broken," but we were thriving in a way we hadn't experienced before. I realized I no longer watched the clock or counted the hours. I no longer tried to make sure the "family" and the "mission" columns added up. I no longer felt like a bystander of the mission. And Mike felt like he had more time with the family.

WE INCLUDED more people in our life, to help us in the little things and the big things, in our family and in our mission.

We were no longer managing boundaries and margins, because people were simply with us in all of life, helping us with the things we needed help with (which was a lot of things, by the way!). Our ministry and family life were thriving in new ways because there were simply more hands to do the work and more giftedness for the tasks at hand, and we were actually investing in people to develop them as disciples of Jesus. We had stumbled upon a new way of functioning.

WE WERE no longer managing boundaries and margins, because people were simply with us in all of life.

As these people simply helped us do our life together, we shared whatever wisdom we had somehow gained in our journey, and we began to disciple them. We didn't get them into an extensive program in church—we simply discipled them "along the way," over meals, family prayers, laundry, carpooling, and bedtime stories. The remarkable thing is that they stayed around. They simply became part of our family! Our little nuclear family was becoming an extended family. Some of them are still with us. We were learning what it looked like to be a **family ON mission**.

At the beginning, we had simply said, "Come walk with us. Sometimes we'll be moving fast, so you may have to run at times, but you're welcome to come with us." No one seemed to mind when we had to run. We were **moving as a pack**, moving forward, gathering up others as we traveled toward what God had called us to do. Making disciples this way led us to discover **Family on Mission**.

What it means is that when we move forward in mission, we do it together if at all possible. Together with our kids, together with those we are discipling, together with those whom we simply can't seem to get rid of! We're going to involve each other and our kids in anything and everything involving our life and mission. As much as possible, we involve everyone in everything.

After our time in Brixton, we had a brief sabbatical in Arkansas before we moved back to England, to work in a church in Sheffield called St. Thomas. What emerged from that wonderful time of rest and recreation was a more defined process that we now call being a **Family on Mission**.

Our children have been raised with this. They know no other way. They know only how to be in an extended family. They laugh about how the instinct in every situation is to always do it with others, to do it in community. When we need to go to the grocery store for a gallon of milk, we usually end up with a whole carload of people going, making it into an adventure. Our children did well in school by drawing on the combined skills and intelligence of those around them. They have a wide knowledge of many cultures that they would never have seen if we had stayed simply within our nuclear family.

We told them very clearly that they didn't need to wait until they were adults to be part of what God had called us to do, that they were completely included and a vital part of now. And they thrived on that. They are actually still part of what we are called to do today. They now work with Mike and me as part of 3DM. We have failed many times in parenthood and ministry, so we consider it a huge blessing that, after all this, our children still like us and want to be part of our lives.

It seems that one of the things the Holy Spirit is doing in the church and the world in our day is moving us...

- Away from the destructive dichotomy of **Family OR Mission**, where we can do only one or the other

- Away from the Band-Aid fix of **Family AND Mission**, where we keep them separate and try to manage boundaries and margins

- Toward the integrated life of **Family ON Mission**, where we wholeheartedly embrace being part of a covenant community, and with those people play our part in God's kingdom mission.

Family OR Mission crushes us, because we have to sacrifice one thing or the other, while both are necessary if we're going to live out the call of God.

Family AND Mission exhausts us, because we need to manage the boundaries between family and mission. Thus our family life never quite feels purposeful, and our mission life never quite feels natural.

Family ON Mission empowers us, because we learn to live an integrated life, moving forward in mission as a pack, as a covenant family with a kingdom mission.

DISCIPLESHIP AND MISSION

never really work unless we are able to create the *texture* of family on mission.

I want to make it clear that this Family on Mission stuff is not just for people with children or the perfect couple living in the suburbs with the perfect marriage and the perfect life. Family on mission is for single people, divorced people, single parents, couples with no kids, couples with eight kids, empty nesters, teenagers and college students. We are *all* called to function as an integral member of some kind of Family on Mission because this is who God is. That's how Jesus (who was single, by the way) functioned. Our identity is deeply rooted in family because the basic nature of God is family.

The point is that discipleship and mission never really work unless we are able to create the texture of **family on mission**. If we're going to make disciples and move out in mission, we need to go from managing boundaries to integrating family and mission into **one life**, a cohesive framework and fabric that empowers a *culture* of discipleship and mission, not just occasional events and periodic programs.

God has created us for this, and Jesus, our brother and king, will show us how to do it. And to top it all off, the Holy Spirit is leading us to rediscover it right now, and will empower us to do it! Let's dive in.

2
∽ LONGING FOR ∽ FAMILY

A CULTURAL EARTHQUAKE

Mike Writes:

Before we talk about how Family on Mission is rooted in the nature of God himself and what we see in the life of Jesus, we want to take a moment to notice that this is actually a longing that seems to be re-emerging in our culture right now—the longing not just to be part of a family, but also to be part of a family with a mission greater than its own survival.

Anthropologists teach us to look at the artifacts of cultures, because they reveal what the people of that culture think is true and important, what they accept and what they reject, what they long for. When we step back and observe what artifacts our culture is producing (books, movies, television, music, other forms of art), we see a longing for family. And not just a nuclear family (which is a fairly modern experiment that is failing), but the more ancient **extended family**: a relational network of blood and non-blood relationships, natural family along with friends, neighbors, and work relationships. This was the "household" of the ancient world. We have adopted the Greek word for household to refer to this reality: *oikos*.

In some ways the new advertisements from cell phone service provider Sprint have picked up on the idea of *oikos* without realizing it. They have a new cell phone plan that can include both friends *and* family, called the "Framily Plan." We wish we had thought of that word! It's the perfect encapsulation of what we mean when we say *oikos*, and it's how most cultures have lived for most of human history.

We are living in the aftermath of a cultural earthquake that has dominated much of the second half of the twentieth century. Traditional beliefs and customs have been questioned and overturned during this time, and many biological families completely broke down. The young people who survived this upheaval look a lot like survivors of an earthquake: they are shell-shocked and of course deeply suspicious of going back into the systems that crumbled and collapsed on top of them.

They saw the marriages of their parents and their friends' parents fall into petty bickering and eventual divorce. They felt and witnessed the pain of that process—no wonder they delay (and even put off entirely) marriage and having kids. They saw the churches they attended with their parents split several times because of unresolved bitterness—no wonder they don't want to come to church. It doesn't look safe!

The funny thing, though, is that in the midst of the rubble, they still long for family. We can see through the artifacts they produce that they are seeking to rebuild their own extended families out of the pieces that have fallen apart. It seems our culture, despite its suspicions, is attempting to reclaim life in the context of family.

THE EVOLUTION OF THE TV FAMILY

It's interesting to trace how this pursuit of family has evolved over the past few years. In the early 1990s, for example, two of the most popular shows on television were about nuclear families trying to make life work. *Roseanne* was

a sitcom about the Conners, a working-class nuclear family in Illinois, and *Home Improvement* featured the trials and triumphs of the Taylors, a nuclear family in suburban Detroit. Although there were of course various friends and neighbors involved, they were mostly peripheral and supplementary. For example, the Taylors had a neighbor named Wilson who featured in many episodes, but interestingly we only ever saw the top of his head over their backyard fence. I can't remember an episode when he was actually invited into the Taylors' home; he wasn't really part of the fabric of their family. *Roseanne* and *Home Improvement* were essentially about the nuclear family. It's as if both shows were a last gasp at trying to save the failing experiment of the nuclear family existing apart from the support of an extended family (which the name *Home Improvement* suggests).

Then, starting in 1994, another kind of sitcom began to shoot up the charts to occupy some of the top spots for the next ten years. One show in particular began to define family very differently from the Conners and the Taylors. *Friends*.

Friends seems to be a classic Generation X narrative. It was a show about six people living in Manhattan, some related, some not, trying to rebuild a sense of community out of the rubble of their comedically dysfunctional families of origin. Ross and Monica were children of Jewish parents. Ross was his parents' favorite, while Monica was always forgotten and never quite good enough for her mother's standards. Chandler was the product of a "deeply conflicted" parental relationship. His parents announced their divorce to him on Thanksgiving when he was nine years old, which caused him to never celebrate the holiday again.

Phoebe grew up without a father, and her mom committed suicide when she was a teenager. She later finds out the woman who raised her was not actually her mother. Joey is a struggling actor from a large Italian family, whose father has been cheating on his mother for years, but Joey eventually finds out his mother knew all along. Rachel was destined for a life of luxury before walking out on her own wedding and landing somehow with these five friends in New York. Her implacable father, possibly alcoholic mother and two neurotic sisters regularly orbit into the group of friends who slowly become family.

These six people meet in 1994, devoid of any real sense of identity, carrying the scars and wounds of broken families, attempting to rebuild a sense of family with one another. This kind of situation resonates so strongly with our culture that one year later it was one of the top shows on television.

Friends ran for ten seasons, and in the end the six single people who began by trying to forge some sense of community with one another had actually

IN THE END

the six single people who began by trying to forge some sense of community with one another had actually become a new kind of family.

become a new kind of family. It was fascinating to watch the characters as they transitioned from quiet desperation to rooted and realistic hopefulness. By the end, they had re-created an authentic extended family. Some are married; some aren't. There are children in the mix. Phoebe's brother, his wife, and their triplets are recurring characters in the show and are part of the extended family. Rachel's sisters, Gunther, Janice and her husband, the list goes on. *Friends* didn't try to repair the nuclear family; it re-created an extended family out of the rubble of the broken-down nuclear family.

We see this same kind of theme in ABC's current comedy *Modern Family*, which was the number one television comedy starting in 2010 and winner of four straight Emmys for Best Comedy. It's the story of a *very* untraditional family seeking to function as a new kind of extended family in the midst of their brokenness and quirkiness. In the midst of their dysfunction and foibles, they discover they need one another, and life is richer when it is shared even with those who annoy us from time to time. It's another depiction of the power of the extended family that our culture seems to be longing for.

This desire to be part of a larger network of relationships that feel like an extended family seems to be everywhere. We see it in TV shows and movies like *Parenthood*, *Toy Story 3*, and *The Incredibles*. We see it in the entourages that celebrities gather around them—a mix of friends, family, and employees who make up their re-created extended family.

ADVERTISING FAMILY

Perhaps there is no better or more explicit example of our culture's hardwiring for family than in an award-winning Walmart commercial from 2008. In it, an average, young twenty-something is walking around his Christmas party, singing about the people who've come over to his house:

The holidays are here again
So I'm inviting all my friends
The people who are close to me
They're my extended family

You've got my mom, my sis, my brother
My surprisingly cool stepmother
And the two kids that she had
Before she ever met my dad

Next you've got my aunts and cousins
They showed up with several dozen
friends of theirs, It's fine with me;
I've got enough for all

Here in the hall you've got my office mates
My best friend and his online date
They've all come here to celebrate
This is my family!

My judo coach, my allergist
My MySpace friends and Twitter list
And the first girl that I ever kissed
You're beautiful, I love you

'Cause there's one truth I've found
And it's never let me down:
When you stock up on joy,
there's enough to go 'round

Singing: Joy! Enough to go 'round
enough to go 'round and around
and around and around.

Aside from the fact that we're not sure if anyone actually uses MySpace anymore, the interesting thing is that he's identifying his extended family as the "the people who are close to me." Those people include those he is related to by blood, like his mom, siblings, aunts, and cousins, but they also include those who are *not* related, like his judo coach and allergist! They are all at the party on the same footing, enjoying one another's company and being part of the "family."

Barbara Lippert, an ad critic for *Adweek*, called the ad "exactly right for the *zeitgeist*." That word *zeitgeist* simply means the "spirit of the age," which means she was sensing that the ad captured something about the longing most people have for that kind of family. There is something about people re-creating extended family that hits the right chord, that names what our culture wants and already seems to be trying to do.

ZOMBIES SHOW US THE WAY

Most of these cultural artifacts are telling us that people are longing for family, but one place we see the full picture of being a Family *on mission* beginning to crystallize is in AMC's TV drama *The Walking Dead*, which is a show about a zombie apocalypse (yes, you read that correctly). Because of its subject matter and source material (graphic novels that appeal to a very niche audience), the show wasn't expected to be a huge hit. But when the fourth season premiered in the fall of 2013, it was watched by a record-breaking 16.1 million viewers. The show portrays a dystopian world where a viral contagion has infected most of the human population, initially killing them but then reviving them, turning them into "walkers" (zombies who seek to transfer the virus by attacking humans).

The uninfected, if they are isolated in small groups, stand little chance of surviving. So the survivors begin to band together to pool their resources for survival and create a community. Initially everyone is simply trying to survive, and the desperate situation has forced them to come together for mutual protection and provision. But by the end of the third season, a fascinating thing has happened: the group that started as a desperate band of survivors has become a community, an extended family of sorts. But they've become something more than just a family. They've become a family *on mission*. Not just seeking their own survival, but also attempting to reclaim something about what it means to be human and how to flourish in the midst of desperate and horrifying circumstances.

> THEY'VE BECOME **something more that just a family. They've become a family *on mission*.**

The show's popularity is perhaps due to this longing that people have to be part of a family on mission, part of a community that lives and works for a purpose higher than its own survival: an extended family that exists for a mission that is more important than the agenda of any single individual in the family. Family for its own sake is too insular and myopic to carry its own weight. People are longing to be part of a mission that's worth living and dying for, and out of that mission they become part of a family that's worth fighting for. Mission is the integrating principle that binds the family together and makes everything else work.

And while our culture's longings don't necessarily tell us what is true, it's interesting that what our culture seems to be desperate for is *exactly* what God has been seeking to do from the very beginning—gather a family and give them a mission. This is what we explore in the next chapter.

3

∽ WE WERE CREATED ∽ FOR THIS

FROM THE VERY BEGINNING

Mike Writes:

Here's the thing—as the missional conversation has progressed, all of us have learned quite a bit about mission. We emphasize and define mission, we equip people to live on mission, we attempt to help people understand and live out mission practically. If it's about family on mission, we have had a lot of teaching about the *mission* part, but very little about the *family* part. Because of this we end up emphasizing the *activity* of mission and not the *identity* we carry that empowers mission. Essential to our identity in God is that we don't exist as individuals only. Our identity is that we are a family on mission.

This is rooted in the two key themes of the Scriptures: covenant and kingdom. Covenant means that God has called us into a relationship with himself that leads us to become *one* with him. Covenant is two becoming one. That's the **family** part. Kingdom means that our Father who has called us into relationship with himself also happens to have the most important job you can think of: he's the king of the universe. And as the king, he's not looking only for relationship—he's looking for representatives. That's the **mission** part— the same people who are in covenantal relationship with him also adopt his mission and learn to represent his kingship in the world.

Covenant is always about relationship and family. Kingdom is always about representation and mission.

COVENANT IS always about relationship and family. Kingdom is always about representation and mission.

One of our problems, though, is that we oftentimes think of these things as distinct categories. In other words, sometimes you are doing the covenant/family thing and other times you are doing the kingdom/mission thing. But that's not how it works. You can't separate them or compartmentalize them, because they are about your *identity*. They are like the double helix in DNA—it doesn't work unless the two strands are connected to one another. We can't do family sometimes and mission other times. That's the exhausting family AND mission dynamic we talked about in the first chapter. Instead we have to learn to *integrate* covenant and kingdom if we're going to fulfill the call of God. We have to learn to be families ON mission.

This is how God has always worked. Before there was a tabernacle, temple, synagogue, or church, there was a family. Family on mission was how God started his project of creating beings in his image to represent him. Family on mission was how he started his project of saving and redeeming his creation after they fell. Family on mission was how he operated throughout salvation history. And Family on mission was how Jesus functioned in bringing redemption to its climax in his life, death, and resurrection. Let's take a stroll through the Bible to see how these things play out.

GOD IS FAMILY ON MISSION

Even before we go back to the beginning, we need to go back to *before* the beginning. Before we talk about creation, we need to talk about the God who created everything, who existed before creation. We need to look at the nature of God himself to see how this family on mission stuff goes all the way back to who God is, because the nature of God is definitive for those who are made in his image and function in his family.

THIS FAMILY ON MISSION stuff goes all the way back to who God is.

One of the key concepts within the missional conversation over the past few years has been the *missio dei*, which means "the mission of God." This concept has been supremely important in helping to root our missional activity in the nature and activity of God himself. We are on mission because we are created and redeemed by a God who is himself on mission. The *missio dei* emphasis has been long needed and was much welcomed. It meant that our activity was grounded in the activity of God, meaning that we weren't so much doing mission *for* God as doing mission *with* God. This makes all the difference in the world when it comes to missional living.

However, to be honest, I think this has caused some unintended consequences. It's very easy for people to hear all this missional talk and feel guilty about their lack of missional performance. At worst it stirs up guilt that we're "not doing enough," and at best it produces people who have a vague conviction that they should be "missional" at work, at school, in the neighborhood, etc, but who don't really know how to do it in a non-weird way. So we either end up saying and doing awkward things, or we say and do nothing at all (which inspires more guilt!).

We hear the theology of *missio dei* and feel inspired by it, but we end up faltering in our practice, because we lack an identity that could inform a more effective methodology. The primary identity we carry is "individual missionary," and so our methodology becomes individualistic. We are individuals on mission. Think about it—even the most "missional" churches probably do something along these lines: we get together on Sundays to be inspired and encouraged, but when we are sent to go participate in the *missio dei*, **we are sent as individual missionaries**, trying to influence our workplace, struggling to make an impact in our neighborhood, attempting to be a solitary witness to our peers at school. If we're honest, this methodology isn't producing the same kind of fruit as we see in the book of Acts.

In other words, something about the way we conceive think about the *missio dei* is producing the methodology of individual missionaries. When the *missio dei* is combined with the heady cocktail of Western individualism, it inevitably gives rise to an individualistic methodology of mission. **We think through the lens of individuals being sent on mission because we envision God as an individual on mission.**

However, one of the distinctive hallmarks of Christian

SOMETHING ABOUT the way we think about the *missio dei* is producing the identity and methodology of individual missionaries.

faith is that God is not simply an individual. Although we do of course believe that God is one, the New Testament reveals that we see his unity expressed in a diversity of three persons. Within the Mystery that is the unity of the Godhead, there is community.

This community of persons is revealed at the baptism of Jesus, where "heaven was opened, and he saw the Spirit of God descending like a dove and alighting on him. And a voice from heaven said, 'This is my Son, whom I love; with him I am well pleased.'"[2] Note the language of family! There is a Father speaking identity to a Son, and the empowering Spirit of God descending as a dove. This is the Trinity, as it was eventually called by the early church father Tertullian.

The interesting thing about what the Father spoke over Jesus at his baptism — which anyone listening at the time would have recognized — was that they were words of commission, **sending Jesus on official family business.** Paul uses almost the same familial language when he sends Timothy to Corinth on gospel business, "For this reason I have sent to you Timothy, my son whom I love, who is faithful in the Lord."[3]

The revelation at the very beginning of Jesus' ministry is that he is not operating independently, but he is coming from a family to represent a family.

The Trinity isn't simply an abstract concept to be contemplated by spiritual directors and scholars; it's a deeply relational reality that tells us that at the very center of God's nature is community. A family. God is family. And the God who is family is on mission. God himself *is* Family on Mission.

So if our theology ends up defining our methodology, perhaps we need to start emphasizing the Trinity in our talk of *missio dei*.[4] Perhaps it's time to

....

[2] Matthew 3:16-17

[2] 1 Corinthians 4:17

[4] We acknowledge that *missio dei* at its best has always been taught in trinitarian terms, but as the missional conversation has become more and more mainstream, this trinitarian focus has been diluted. As a result, people take the concept of *missio dei* and pour it into the container of Western individualism, thus producing a methodology of sending out individual missionaries.

So while *missio dei* doesn't cause individualistic mission all by itself, it does get co-opted by Western individualism. Thus our suggestion for some nuance and emphasis on Trinity in our talk of mission!

start talking about the *missio trinitatis*, the "mission of the Trinity." As we do, we'll find our methodology shifts from individual missionaries doing the best they can to families on mission who demonstrate and proclaim a fuller picture of who God is.

GOD HIMSELF is Family on Mission.

(Again, in our talk of "family" we are including every human being, not just married people with kids! Family on mission is for single people, married people, kids, adults, empty-nesters, everyone! When we talk about being a family on mission, we believe it's something we are all called to participate in. After all, Jesus was a single man who formed a family with a bunch of people he wasn't related to. More on that later.)

God himself is Family on Mission, which is why, as we'll see, he consistently operates this way in his work with his creation. From Adam and Eve ("it is not good for man to be alone") to Abraham to Jesus to the early church, family on mission is the methodology God has used to accomplish his redemptive work in the world. All of God's missional activity springs from his identity: Family on Mission.

CREATED AS FAMILY

It's out of who God is as Family on Mission that he creates the world, and what we see in his creation is that those who specifically bear his image also function as a family on mission. In the creation poem at the beginning of Genesis, God creates the world. A phrase keeps getting repeated: "God saw that it was good." Everything about God's creation is good, and it is announced after each stage of creation.

Interestingly, though, the first time God says something is *not* good is after he creates the first being made "in his image," Adam, the first human. What does God declare is not good about Adam? "It is not good for the man to be alone," God concludes. **The first thing in all creation that God declares "not good" is a human being alone.**

God remedies the situation by creating the first woman, Eve. The man is now not alone anymore, and Adam and Eve function together in such a deeply interwoven covenant relationship that it's almost as if they are one person.

Genesis calls it "one flesh" and declares that this is how human beings are meant to function together in the image of God. Two become one and function together.

God created a family, and gave them a mission: "Be fruitful and increase in number; fill the earth and subdue it." At a very basic level this task is impossible for a single individual to accomplish! Adam and Eve needed one another to even begin to carry out the mission God had given them. The very first expression of humanity was a family on mission.

From the very beginning, we can see that humans are meant to exist deeply connected in covenant relationship to God *and to each other*, and that this is a vital key to being able to function in the mission God calls us to.

BLESSED TO BE A BLESSING

After Adam and Eve pulled away from their life-giving relationship with God, all creation began to drift from the covenant and call God had given. Sin entered the world, and one of the first results was the violation and severing of family—Adam and Eve's son Cain murders his brother Abel in a fit of jealous rage. Humans called to function as a family on mission begin to move in the very opposite direction: violating covenant relationships instead of honoring them and living selfishly for their own benefit instead of surrendering to the mission of God.

Astonishingly, God refuses to abandon his creation that has rebelled against him, and promises that he will actually do the work of saving and redeeming them. One day a descendent of Adam and Eve will crush the head of the serpent that tempted them in the first place. But how?

Years pass, and God continues to interact with and woo his creation. After the great flood he works with Noah and his family, giving them a mission: "Be fruitful and increase in number and fill the earth." (Where have we heard that before?) They do so, and once again there are multitudes of humans living, working and playing on Earth.

HE STARTED WITH a family and gave them a mission.

But God knew he needed to do more to secure salvation

for his creation. So when the time was right, and he was ready to act on his promise to save the world, he started with a family and gave them a mission. He called Abram to leave his home, his people, and his father's household, and go to the "land that I will show you." God promised that he would bless Abram (who was an old man with no children) and make him into a great nation, and that "all peoples on earth will be blessed through you." Abram takes his wife Sarai and his nephew Lot and they leave everything that had given them identity and security, and set off for a land that will be shown to them.

FAMILY ON MISSION
is God's
methodology
for saving the
world.

Thus God starts his massive project of saving the world by calling a family and giving them a mission. He will continue to work with this family as it grows into a nation (which is really just a tribe of families), and eventually from this family will come one who fulfills all that God has planned for his creation. The fascinating thing, though, is that God begins this huge project in such a small way, with a family. **Family on mission is God's methodology for saving the world.**

CALLED TO FUNCTION IN FAMILY

In the unfolding revelation of Scripture we see that the God who is a community in unity is expressing the same reality in the creatures who bear his image. From before the beginning on through the entire story of the Old Testament, we see family on mission at work in the plans of God, because it is simply a reflection of who he is as God—community in unity, family on mission.

This is a strong contrast to the message our culture has been promoting for at least a few hundred years, that you can be your "best you" as an individual, on your own. That somehow all God wants to do in you and through you is mainly just a matter of a private transaction between him and you, with brief interactions with other people when you go to church.

Instead, we are called to function together as families on mission. These relationships aren't just loose friendships or the kinds of connections we cultivate at networking events. These aren't just business partnerships or friendly acquaintances. It must be much deeper than that. To really lean into the dreams God has put into our hearts, we need to learn how to live as families on mission again, because this is simply how God works in the world. As theologian Gerhard Lohfink writes:

> It can only be that God begins in a small way, at one single place in the world. There must be a place, visible, tangible, where the salvation of the world can begin: that is, where the world becomes what it is supposed to be according to God's plan. Beginning at that place, the new thing can spread abroad, but not through persuasion, not through indoctrination, not through violence. Everyone must have the opportunity to come and see. All must have the chance to behold and test this new thing. Then, if they want to, they can allow themselves to be drawn into the history of salvation that God is creating. Only in that way can their freedom be preserved. What drives them to the new thing cannot be force, not even moral pressure, but only the fascination of a world that is changed.[5]

Coming into contact with a family on mission is how people become fascinated by "a world that is changed." Family on Mission is how God has been working since the creation of the world and it's how he's working today. We human beings are hardwired for family, and until we embrace that reality, we will always have a stunted, frustrated experience as Christians. It's in our DNA. It's who God has created us to be. We are meant to exist in family.

DID JESUS DO FAMILY ON MISSION?

THERE MUST BE **a place, visible, tangible, where the salvation of the world can begin.**

So if this is true, we would expect to see Jesus functioning this way. If he is the supreme revelation of who God is (and he is),[6] then we'd expect him to reveal this reality as well. We would expect him to build a family on mission to fulfill his missional call. And yet often we think of him as the consummate individual. After all, even though he was sent by the Father, doesn't he operate as an individual on mission?

---

[5] Gerhard Lohfink, *Does God Need the Church?* p. 27.
[6] "Anyone who has seen me has seen the Father" (John 14:9).

This is an important question because Jesus is always our model. Everything we do in discipleship and mission needs to find its way back to something about the way Jesus did things, or it isn't normative. Is family on mission simply a convenient ministry strategy or is it integrated into the way Jesus functioned in his mission?

What we'll see is that Jesus refused to do his ministry apart from the context of family on mission. When he began his ministry, he started by calling a group of disciples to be with him to become his family, and he sent them as a family on mission.

4

✎ JESUS LOOKS ✎ FOR A FAMILY

THE WAY OF JESUS

Mike Writes:

There are at least two good reasons to dive deeply into the life of Jesus as we think about what it means to live as a family on mission. First, if everything we've said so far is true, that God is family on mission and has always operated through families on mission, and Jesus is the full revelation of what God is really like, we'd expect to see family on mission in his life and ministry. If we don't see family on mission in Jesus, it must mean we're not seeing the other stuff clearly, and we need to rethink it all. How did he do the things he did? Do we see him building a family on mission?

Second, as disciples of Jesus, we must pay attention to the *way* he did things. Too often, we disregard the *way* he did things as incidental and unimportant for our lives. We listen to his word, we practice his works, but if we don't also imitate his *ways* we usually end up moving in the wrong direction. Since we are his disciples, our default posture should be to seek to emulate his way of doing things. One of the first questions we answer when we encounter a new situation is, "How did Jesus do it?" Instead of WWJD ("What Would Jesus Do?"), we could call it WDJD: "What Did Jesus Do?"

WORD

WORKS   WAY

It's not just about hearing the words of Jesus and doing the works of Jesus—it's about operating in the way of Jesus. Since Jesus reveals to us what God is really like, his word is authoritative for us, his works are definitive, and his way is normative. What is the way of Jesus? Why did he do what he did and can we learn from him how to build and live as a family on mission?

To answer these questions, we're going to look at the ministry of Jesus from multiple angles, editing together scenes from the four Gospels that give us different perspectives on what Jesus was doing during the course of his ministry.

REDEFINING FAMILY

Sometimes we forget how downright shocking some of the things were that Jesus said and did! There's an especially scandalous scene shortly after Jesus begins his ministry that gives us a picture of what he was doing in terms of building a family on mission.

Because of Jesus' miracles and teaching, large crowds are following him. People are beginning to ask whether he might be the Messiah, the one who will save them from their enemies. Jesus is upsetting many in the religious establishment by performing many of the functions people would normally need to go to the Temple for, like forgiveness and healing. All the same, multitudes are following him, hanging on his every word.

So it is more of the same when one day Jesus goes to someone's household (*oikos*) and a huge crowd gathers to listen to him. "He and his disciples were not even able to eat," Mark's Gospel says. "When his family heard about this, they went to take charge of him, for they said, 'He is out of his mind.'"

Imagine the scene for a moment. Jesus has begun his ministry, but it's so unexpected and controversial that his own family members are somewhat embarrassed about it and concerned for him. They thought he had gone crazy. In the language and culture of the day, they are voicing what many of the Jewish leaders had begun saying, that Jesus was being influenced by a demon. He needed help, and his family has come to take charge of him.

Jesus' mother and brothers arrive outside the house, but they can't get in because of all the people. They send a message in, and someone tells

Jesus, "Your mother and brothers are outside looking for you." Jesus' response is utterly shocking: "Who are my mother and my brothers?" He looks at those seated around him in a circle and says, "Here are my mother and my brothers! Whoever does God's will is my brother and sister and mother."[7]

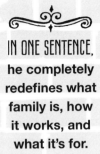

IN ONE SENTENCE,
he completely
redefines what
family is, how
it works, and
what it's for.

This would have been so astonishing to first-century Jews that they would have never forgotten it. They would be telling this story for years. It sounds shocking today, but back then it would have been utterly mind-boggling to think that anyone would say such a thing. He tells his mother and brothers that he has a new family now. Can you imagine telling your mother such a thing? So much for focusing on the family! In one fell swoop, Jesus overturns everything they thought they knew about family. His disciples weren't just his roadies or work associates—they are his family. For Jesus, making disciples is about building a family. **In one sentence, he completely redefines what family is, how it works, and what it's for.**

For Jesus, family means something much bigger than what we normally think of. So how did he arrive there? How did this happen? Let's go back to the beginning and find out.

STRAGGLERS AND TAGALONGS

At Jesus' baptism, the Trinity is revealed, and his identity is confirmed: he is sent from a family to represent a family. Specifically the family of the Trinity, the household of heaven. After his baptism Jesus goes into the wilderness to be tempted by the devil. This is where his identity will be tested in all the same ways Adam and Eve were tested. In fact, the temptations Jesus faces in the desert are the main ways each of us will be challenged on our identity. But that's another book!

Jesus successfully resists temptation, triumphing where Adam and Eve failed. The result is that Jesus returns to Galilee "in the power of the Spirit."

....

[7] See this story in Mark 3:20-35.

News spreads quickly that something truly remarkable is happening. Jesus is teaching powerfully in the synagogues, and everyone marvels at his words.

Luke's Gospel tells us that Jesus makes his way to Nazareth at this point. Why? Very likely because that's where his family was from. He knows his identity. He knows what he was called to do. He had been tested and tried and found true. It was time to begin, but he knows what everyone knew in that time—that you can't actually function without an *oikos*, without a family to be on mission with you. For Jesus, the most natural first place to look for his family is among his blood relatives in his hometown.

Going toward Nazareth meant he would walk past the place where his relative John was still baptizing people. As Jesus passes by, the Fourth Gospel tells us that John cries out, "Behold, the Lamb of God!" Andrew and another disciple hear him say this and decide to follow Jesus, leaving John the Baptist. The other disciple is likely the eventual Apostle John, as scholars point out that when authors refer to themselves, they often use self-effacing language, choosing not to name themselves. So Andrew and John are now literally following Jesus on foot.

It's a funny scene to imagine. Jesus is walking on the road toward Nazareth with two potential disciples hot on his heels, perhaps hanging back a bit so they don't look too eager, but all the same wanting Jesus to notice they're there. Jesus looks behind him and sees these two men following him and asks, "What do you want?" Andrew and John seem almost sheepish in their answer, unsure of what to say. "Rabbi," they say, "where are you staying?" It's almost as if they had become embarrassed boys, asking a silly question, "Where you goin', mister?"

JESUS DOESN'T
schedule a special meeting for these two; he simply invites them into what he's already doing.

Jesus recognizes they want to follow him and see if he really is the one John the Baptist claims he is, and offers a tender invitation, "Come and see." Jesus doesn't schedule a special meeting for these two; he simply invites them into what he's already doing. He knows where he is going, but he makes room for these two tagalongs to see what might unfold. They accept the invitation and spend the day with Jesus. Eventually they pick up a fisherman named Simon, and two others named Philip and Nathanael, Jesus and five tagalongs are journeying toward Nazareth.

From there, Jesus continues to travel north. It may very well be that he first stops by Cana. It's a good walk from Nazareth, but not too far away and it looks like there's a family wedding there. In those days, family weddings were enormously important because one extended family was uniting with another extended family. You may know the story, but at this wedding in Cana, a few of Jesus' disciples are there, as well as his mother, and he transforms a potentially devastating wedding disaster into the best party any of them have ever been to. Who saves the best wine until last, after all?

REJECTED AT NAZARETH

He eventually makes it back to Nazareth and on the Sabbath goes to the synagogue, where he would have been surrounded by his extended family, along with friends and neighbors he has known for years. He also would very likely sit with the people of his trade, which would have been the same as that of his father Joseph—a builder.

Traditionally we think of Jesus as a carpenter, but the original word is more accurately translated "builder." The job was more akin to a modern-day contractor than to a carpenter. Builders build with the material available to them, of course, and in those days the building material most readily available was stone, not wood. The picture that emerges is that Jesus was more of a stonemason than a carpenter. He was a builder and he used stone to build. It could be that Jesus actually worked quite a bit in the rebuilding of a nearby town called Sepphoris, which had been destroyed by the Romans because of a rebellion just before Jesus was born. To demonstrate what Rome does to traitors, after they burned the city they sold many of its inhabitants into slavery and crucified two thousand Jewish rebels.

So it's the Sabbath, and Jesus would have been sitting with the builders in the synagogue, surrounded by his extended family and friends who've known him almost his entire life. During this particular meeting he stands up to speak. This would have been a fairly normal practice—anyone was welcome to speak in a synagogue meeting. He takes a scroll, unrolls it to a section from the prophet Isaiah, and begins to read.

"The Spirit of the Lord is on me,
    because he has anointed me
    to proclaim good news to the poor.
He has sent me to proclaim freedom for the prisoners
    and recovery of sight for the blind,
to set the oppressed free,
    to proclaim the year of the Lord's favor."

Everyone nods in agreement. These would have been incredibly popular and comforting words about the Messiah, the anointed leader of Israel who would come and bring salvation and deliverance from their enemies. The synagogue waits with bated breath to hear what this local boy might have to say about this passage that they haven't already heard from their rabbis.

"Today this scripture is fulfilled in your hearing," Jesus says. He goes on to talk about his mission that scandalously includes the *Gentiles*, of all people! Jesus is there among his family and friends, but he is stating the missional purpose toward which his life is oriented. He is declaring the *mission* of his family, because he knows it can't be a family oriented around any old mission. The missional purpose of the family he would gather must be crystal clear, and so he makes sure everyone knows what his life is going to be all about. This is my mission, Jesus says—to do this Isaiah 61 stuff for everyone, Jews and Gentiles included!

Jesus teaches this and at the same time reveals the hearts of his hearers: "Surely you will quote this proverb to me: 'Physician, heal yourself!' And you will tell me, 'Do here in your hometown what we have heard that you did in Capernaum.' Truly I tell you, no prophet is accepted in his hometown. I assure you that there were many widows in Israel in Elijah's time, when the sky was shut for three and a half years and there was a severe famine throughout the land. Yet Elijah was not sent to any of them, but to a widow in Zarephath in the region of Sidon. And there were many in Israel with leprosy in the time of Elisha the prophet, yet not one of them was cleansed—only Naaman the Syrian."

HE IS DECLARING the *mission* of his family.

In other words, "You assume that because we're related by blood that you'll get privileged status, an inside track on what God is up to, but that's not how God works."

It doesn't go over well. "Did he just claim to be the Messiah?" they wonder. Did he just include the Gentiles in God's people? The news has come to them that he is an amazing teacher and is even able to heal the sick with a command and drive out demons with a word. And he has the gall to come to his hometown and preach this kind of sermon? Isn't this Joseph's son? Don't we know his family? Didn't we watch him grow up in front of our eyes? Who does he think he is?

IT DOESN'T GO OVER WELL. **Did he just include the Gentiles in God's people?**

This infuriates the group gathered at the synagogue, stirring up their religious exclusivism and nationalism. Not only does Jesus have the gall to claim he is the long-awaited Messiah, but he also tries to redefine what it means! They want to be free from under the thumb of their Gentile rulers, and this *kid* they've known their whole lives has the impudence to tell them that he's a prophet and that they've got it all wrong.

They are now seething with anger at him, and they drive him out of the synagogue, out of Nazareth, and take him to the brow of the hill on which the town was built *in order to throw him off the cliff*. It was a way of killing people. You'd bind them hand and foot and throw them headfirst into a pit, or off a cliff, where the fall would either kill them or knock them unconscious. Then you'd throw large stones at their head until they were dead. It's called "stoning to death," and it's for heretics and sinners. This is what they were about to do to Jesus.

Let's be clear. There are no reports of Jesus' mother clinging to him in an attempt to get the crowd to stop. The text does not say that his brothers were bravely defending him. Sometimes what hurts more than your enemies hating you is your friends and family remaining silent in a time of need. You can imagine the level of rejection that Jesus felt in this moment. These are his family and friends. His brothers, sisters, cousins, aunts, uncles, schoolmates and childhood friends. His colleagues and feasting buddies from way back. He's been with them his whole life and is now thirty years old. These were the people he'd grown up with, people he loved. People he intended to recruit into his family on mission. This is rejection of the deepest kind.

The Bible says that Jesus "walked through the crowd and went on his way," and we're not exactly sure how that happened, but we are certain that his family and friends weren't successful in their attempt to kill him. It was also clear to Jesus that this was no longer his home. These people were not to be his family on mission. They had rejected him in the most vehement way.

Now what? What would he do after this ultimate rejection? Would he swear off family in bitterness and attempt to accomplish his mission alone? Would he give up on his mission to win back his family's good graces?

5

ᔖ JESUS BUILDS ᔖ
A NEW FAMILY

STARTING OVER WITH FRIENDS

Mike Writes:

The most natural place for Jesus to begin to find his family on mission has now firmly rejected him. He has been thrown out of the *oikos* he has been part of his whole life. What is he to do? Remember that Jesus operates in the same way a normal human being operates. He doesn't "know everything" because he's God. He is functioning in the same way he trains us to function. Having experienced a powerful calling in the river and testing in the desert, he is forced to endure a violent rejection in his hometown. What's his next move?

Interestingly, the thing he *doesn't* do is walk off and assume he could do it by himself. He lost his *oikos*, but he doesn't foolishly assume that now he is called to function without one. No, he knows that he needs a family to join him on his mission. *Even the Son of God needed a family to function fully in his calling.*

But where does he turn next? Where does he start looking to find a family to be on mission with him? Nazareth is a *very* closed door, and they are the people he has known his whole life. What's next?

The Bible says that after this he went down to Capernaum. Why would he do that?

EVEN THE SON of God needed a family to function fully in his calling.

JESUS WAS ALSO using the person of peace strategy to find his own family on mission.

Because that's where his new friends are from! Remember the tagalongs he met at the beginning of the journey? The ones who tagged along and were interested in hanging out with him? They spent the whole day with Jesus. They may have even come with him all the way to Nazareth. Andrew and Simon live in Capernaum, and it seems Jesus chooses to go there next for that reason. They seem like people of peace to him.

"Person of peace" is a term Jesus talks with his disciples about later in Luke's Gospel when he sends out seventy-two people on a mission. He tells them that they'll be able to recognize openness to their message when they recognize a person of peace, which Jesus describes as someone who "receives your peace," allows you to stay in his home and feeds you. In other words, someone who likes you, listens to you, welcomes you, and serves you.

Jesus was also using the person of peace strategy to find his family on mission. He looks at this ragtag group of people he can't seem to get rid of. He knows they like him—otherwise, they wouldn't have spent the day with him. He knows they listen to him—they call him "rabbi" and are receptive to his teaching. Now it's time to see whether they'll welcome him and serve him.

It's utterly fascinating to watch Jesus do this in the Gospels. We will follow Luke's ordering of events. He goes to Capernaum because his potential people of peace live there. He starts in the synagogue again, but thankfully gets a different response from the one he got in Nazareth. Nobody tries to kill him this time. Instead "they were amazed at his teaching, because his words had authority." Word begins to spread quickly throughout the region that something remarkable is happening.

Then Jesus leaves the synagogue and goes to the home of Simon and Andrew. They have **welcomed him** into their home. Another sign that they might be true people of peace. Jesus heals Simon's mother-in-law of a fever and she gets up and begins serving them. (Always a good move, healing a mother-in-law. Otherwise nobody in the house would have eaten because clearly the *men* had no idea how to prepare the food.) That evening, people who were sick came to Jesus, and he healed every single one.

News spreads like wildfire, and soon it's difficult for Jesus to go anywhere without attracting huge crowds. One day he's walking by the shore of the Sea of Galilee, where the fishing vessels are moored. As he walks past the water, he sees fishermen in their boats and on the key, mending their nets. He notices Simon and his family and partners there as well, and decides to calibrate a little invitation and challenge with them to see how they'll respond. He needs to see if they'll **serve** him, showing themselves to be true people of peace.

(It's important to note that Jesus doesn't try to force them to serve him. He doesn't cajole or manipulate or twist their arms. He simply asks and then looks for the response. As we seek to identify people of peace, it's important we keep this in mind. Jesus is never about coercion; he's simply observing, looking for people who serve him, because he knows this means his Father is at work in their lives.)

The crowd is pressing around him and suddenly it's a tricky situation to navigate. He gets Simon's attention and says, "Lend me your boat." You have to understand, this wasn't a normal question. A fisherman's boat was an extremely valuable investment that represented his whole livelihood. It's like saying, "Let me use the money in your bank account for a day. I'll give it right back, but I need it for something." It's a big request! Simon agrees, and Jesus has him put the boat out a ways from the shore so he can use it as a natural amplification system to speak to the crowd. They are **serving** Jesus, putting their possessions at the disposal of his mission.

FROM FRIENDS TO FOLLOWERS

Jesus knows they are people of peace, or *friends*—people who know who Jesus is and are friendly toward him. They like hanging out with him and love having him in their home. They enjoy listening to him and think he makes really good points in every sermon they've heard him preach. They are also happy to serve him when they can, letting him use their boat as a portable, floating ampitheater.

But while relationships typically start in that place, you can't build a family if you don't take it any further. So Jesus begins to press into the question of whether they'll go from being friends to followers. Friends serve when they

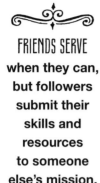

when they can, but followers submit their skills and resources to someone else's mission.

can, but followers submit their skills and resources to someone else's mission.

At the end of his talk in the boat, Jesus takes it one step further by casually suggesting to Simon, "Put out into deep water and let down the nets for a catch." Think about that. Jesus' work experience in his father's *oikos* was in building, not fishing. And now he has become an itinerant teacher and healer. Why would a seasoned fisherman listen to advice from someone who clearly doesn't have any experience fishing?

But Jesus wants to see how Simon will respond, because he needs to see if these are the people who will become part of his family on mission, part of the household he is establishing that will change the world. So he asks Simon to put out the nets in deeper waters.

Simon answers, "Master, we've worked hard all night and haven't caught anything. **But because you say so, I will let down the nets for a catch.**" They are following him now, listening to his instructions even when they're pretty sure they know better. The result is that they catch so many fish that their nets begin to break. They call to their partners to bring another boat, and both are so full of fish that they begin to sink.

In the midst of the chaos, Simon falls to his knees, right there on top of the fish, probably sinking into them a bit. "Go away from me, Lord; I am a sinful man!" he cries, fish flopping all around him. He is astonished at the catch and realizes something more than meets the eye is happening, and it disturbs him to the core.

Jesus has seen what he needs to see—these fishermen have gone from being friends to followers and are on the road to becoming his family on mission. "Don't be afraid," Jesus says, "from now on you will fish for people." In other words, follow me and I will take everything you are and know how to do, embrace it, and transform it for the purposes of my kingdom. They all pull their boats up on shore, leave everything, and follow Jesus.

Within weeks, the boat that was overflowing with fish becomes a household overflowing with people. Jesus has entered Simon's *oikos* and transformed it from a fishing-for-fish enterprise into a fishing-for-people enterprise, and it quickly becomes the epicenter of Jesus' ministry. People gathered in such large numbers that there is no room left, not even outside the door. There often isn't even time to eat. People are pushing aside all the normal boundaries of propriety in their desire to get in on the kingdom that is breaking in through the ministry of Jesus.

The crippled and diseased come to him and he heals them. One time, some men even resort to removing some of the tiles on the roof of one of the buildings and lowering their paralyzed friend down to Jesus, desperate to take advantage of Jesus' presence in their hometown. The *oikos* of common fishermen in Capernaum has become the place where God was visiting his people.

FROM FOLLOWERS TO FAMILY

But there is one more progression to make. The disciples have gone from being friends to followers, and it has transformed everything. They have invited Jesus into their lives, their *oikos*, and made all their skills and resources available to him. **But there is a difference between inviting Jesus into your oikos and becoming part of Jesus' oikos.**

Friends are those who serve the cause when they can. **Followers are those who submit** their skills and resources to have Jesus transform them. But **family are those who surrender** completely, laying down their agenda fully for the agenda of Jesus. This is what the disciples eventually do.

Jesus seems to stay in Capernaum for a while, using Simon's *oikos* as his base of operations, but eventually he begins to move out into the other towns, and his disciples come with him, leaving their transformed *oikos* to join Jesus in his mission, wherever it might take them. They "leave their nets" and join Jesus. It's difficult to underestimate the gravity of this decision for the disciples. Leaving their nets means leaving a livelihood that has probably been passed down for many generations. Leaving their *oikos* means not only abandoning security and provision, but also abandoning their family identity and joining Jesus in his *oikos* that he is building. This is a big decision.

They are beginning the journey of joining Jesus' family, which means being covenantally connected to him, but also becoming part of the work of his *oikos*, his family business.

Here's how it happens.[8] He takes his disciples to Caesarea Philippi, which doesn't sound like that big of a deal to us, but for the disciples, this would have been a bit scandalous. Caesarea Philippi was likely one of the most evil places they could imagine. Although it was only twenty-five miles from Galilee, it had become a den of idolatry and the grossest kinds of immorality. The worst kinds of sin were perpetrated here on a regular basis in honor of the Greek god Pan. There was a cave at the base of a cliff that had spring water flowing out of it, and the inhabitants of the city thought this cave was an entrance to the underworld. They believed that their city was literally a portal to the underworld—the gates of Hades.

As Jesus is walking around this region with his disciples, he asks them, "Who do the people say I am?" It's important to remember that, in this culture, identity is not an individualistic thing that is rooted in one's own internal world. Instead, individual identity is always expressed in the context of community. Identity names not only who someone is, but also what his or her place is in a community. The disciples begin to think back over what they've heard people say: "Some say John the Baptist; others say Elijah; and still others, Jeremiah or one of the prophets."

"But what about you?" Jesus asks them. "Who do you say I am?" What is Jesus looking for here? Remember he is functioning as the head of the Father's household here on earth. As the eldest son, he serves as the "surrogate parent" of God's family on earth. He has the Holy Spirit with him, helping him to see all that the Father is doing, because it's the Father's will that he is here to fulfill. He is building a family, gathering children into the Father's household.

> THEY BELIEVED **that their city was literally a portal to the underworld— the gates of Hades.**

Simon speaks up at this point. "You are the Messiah, the Son of the living God." This is the response Jesus is looking for! "Blessed are you, Simon son of Jonah,"

---

[8] You can find this account in Matthew 16:13-20.

he says, "for this was not revealed to you by flesh and blood, but by my Father in heaven. And I tell you that you are Peter (which means "rock," so we could call him "Rocky"), and on this rock I will build my church, and the gates of Hades will not overcome it. I will give you the keys of the kingdom of heaven; whatever you bind on earth will be bound in heaven, and whatever you loose on earth will be loosed in heaven."

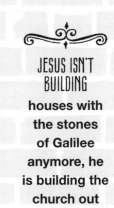

JESUS ISN'T BUILDING houses with the stones of Galilee anymore, he is building the church out of rough-cut jagged stones like Peter.

Jesus calls Simon blessed, first because his answer indicates that the Father has revealed the true identity of Jesus to Simon, meaning that they are called to be part of the same family, to share a name, to be in covenant. So Jesus renames Simon, calling him Peter, which means "rock," which is a name often used for God himself in the Old Testament. On this rock, Jesus says, he will build his church, and the gates of Hades won't prevail against it. I'm sure the disciples at this point looked toward the cave at the base of the cliff and thought, "We're going to be attacking *that place?*"

Notice that Jesus' first move is to join the *oikos* of fishermen and transform it, making them into fishers of people. This brought the disciples from friends to followers. But now Jesus finalizes their move from followers to family by having them join his *oikos*. Remember that Jesus is a builder—that's his trade. And builders build with the material available to them. Peter has just **surrendered** to Jesus and his mission, and Jesus says, "That's great! You are now the raw material that I will shape, and you'll also become a builder like me." Jesus isn't building houses with the stones of Galilee anymore; he is building the church out of rough-cut jagged stones like Peter.

THE FISHERMAN BECOMES A BUILDER

From this point on, Peter is a builder. He has completely surrendered to the vision and values of Jesus' *oikos*. He has completely laid down his old agenda and plan and has given himself completely to Jesus. Peter is a rock being shaped by Jesus the builder, and he becomes a builder himself, shaping others in the way of Jesus.

Peter consistently describes himself in builder language from that point on, except one time, after the resurrection, when he is depressed because of his denial of Jesus. He goes fishing just once more because he isn't sure if he can really be reinstated into Jesus' *oikos* of builders. Jesus graciously reinstates Peter anyway, of course, and he becomes the rock among the apostles that he is called to be.

From that point on, he is a builder because Jesus made him into one. It seems all Peter wants to talk about is bricks and stones and mortar and buildings. Filled with the Holy Spirit during an interrogation in front of the rulers of his people, he boldly states, "Rulers and elders of the people! If we are being called to account today for an act of kindness shown to a man who was lame and are being asked how he was healed, then know this, you and all the people of Israel: It is by the name of Jesus Christ of Nazareth, whom you crucified but whom God raised from the dead, that this man stands before you healed. Jesus is

> "'the stone you builders rejected,
>   which has become the cornerstone.'
>
> "Salvation is found in no one else, for there is no other name under heaven given to mankind by which we must be saved."[9]

In other words, a crippled man was healed because I carry the name of Jesus Christ of Nazareth. I share his identity because I share his name. I'm the little rock, and he's the big rock that you builders rejected, that has now become the capstone.

Then in his first letter, Peter talks about joining the family of God in builder language.

> As you come to him, the living Stone—rejected by humans but chosen by God and precious to him—you also, like living stones, are being built into a spiritual house to be a holy priesthood, offering spiritual sacrifices acceptable to God through Jesus Christ. For in Scripture it says:

....

[9] Acts 4:8-12

"See, I lay a stone in Zion,
  a chosen and precious cornerstone,
and the one who trusts in him
  will never be put to shame."

Now to you who believe, this stone is precious. But to those who do not believe,

"The stone the builders rejected
  has become the cornerstone,"
and,

"A stone that causes people to stumble
  and a rock that makes them fall."

They stumble because they disobey the message--which is also what they were destined for.

But you are a chosen people, a royal priesthood, a holy nation, God's special possession, that you may declare the praises of him who called you out of darkness into his wonderful light. Once you were not a people, but now you are the people of God; once you had not received mercy, but now you have received mercy.[10]

You become part of the family by surrendering your agenda and joining God's *oikos*. Peter tells his readers that they are all included in this! The amazing news is that it wasn't just a limited time offer for Peter and a few others. The reality is that Jesus' intention was to fill his Father's house with children, and that's why he trained his disciples to make disciples, and why he made Peter into a builder who built others into the spiritual house he was building.

Peter is not only a member of the family, but he is also part of the family business. He's a builder now, and he wants everyone else to join him in the same deal. He

> **YOU BECOME PART of the family by surrendering your agenda and joining God's deal.**

....

[10] 1 Peter 2:4-10

has gone from being an observer watching Jesus...

- To a friend who served Jesus
- To a follower who submitted to Jesus
- To a family member who surrendered to Jesus

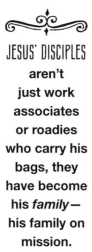

JESUS' DISCIPLES **aren't just work associates or roadies who carry his bags, they have become his *family*— his family on mission.**

Because the other disciples have done the same, Jesus has established an *oikos*, he has built a family on mission to reflect the household of heaven that he represents. This family on mission will be trained to make disciples of all people groups, baptizing them into the identity of the Trinity, and training them to obey everything Jesus said. It all started with a family on mission, and it is advanced through family on mission.

Which brings us back to the story we started this chapter with, putting an exclamation point on this process, highlighting what has been happening in all the conversations and journeys.

Jesus' mother and brothers come to take charge of him, because they assume that he has gone insane. They can't get into the house because it's filled to overflowing again, so they send in a message and someone tells Jesus his mother and brothers are outside looking for him. Jesus shocks his listeners by saying that the people who are related to him by blood are actually not his family anymore. Pointing to his disciples, he said, "Here are my mother and brothers." Jesus' disciples aren't just work associates or roadies who carry his bags, they have become his *family*—**his family on mission**.

FROM A FAMILY TO GROW THE FAMILY

Jesus is sent from the household of heaven to represent the mission of a God who is Family on Mission. He is the Son of a Father, sent from a family to represent a family. After being brutally rejected by his biological family and the relatives he has known his whole life, he gathers a ragtag group of fishermen and others and re-establishes a family on mission to represent his Father.

You could say Jesus is expanding the heavenly family! He is the eldest son, but he is now calling his disciples his brothers, all of whom have the same

Father as him. It's remarkable: Jesus is creating a family, and the mission of the family is to invite more people into the family.

This becomes the mission of the family that Jesus establishes, and even after he ascends to heaven the mission continues. As more disciples are made, the family expands and multiplies, and we rejoice that "both the one who makes people holy and those who are made holy are of the same family. So Jesus is not ashamed to call them brothers and sisters."[11]

AS WE MAKE **disciples and mobilize God's people for mission, the methodology we use must be congruent with the way of Jesus.**

Family on mission is what God has always *been*, and what he has always been *about*. He is our Father, Jesus is our brother, and we are now part of his big family.

This is essentially the strategy that the early church uses in their early missionary journeys. We see Paul eventually moving to a strategy of planting the gospel directly in the Greco-Roman *oikos*, bypassing entirely the traditional religious structure of the synagogue. He simply trained households to live as families on mission, and sociologist Rodney Stark tells us that this is most likely why the Christian faith spread like wildfire in the first few hundred years of the church's history.[12]

This is the adventure we are invited to go on! We get the thrill and challenge of establishing a family on mission so that God's family can continue to grow. As we make disciples and mobilize God's people for mission, the *methodology* we use must be congruent with the way of Jesus. We need to learn how to do **family on mission**.

The good news is that Jesus will teach us how to do it, through the pictures of his life we have in the Gospels as well as his day-by-day leading that comes through the Holy Spirit. The next chapters will dive into the practical realities of what it looks like to build a family on mission today.

---

[11] Hebrews 2:11

[12] You can read the fascinating account in Stark's book *The Rise of Christianity*.

6

✤ BEGINNING TO BUILD ✤
A FAMILY ON MISSION

FAMILY ON MISSION TODAY

Mike Writes:

We've seen that God has always been about Family on Mission. He *is* Family on Mission in his very nature (unity and community in the Trinity), and he has always called families and given them his mission. Jesus' entire ministry was about him being sent from a family to re-establish the family of God around himself. We saw how he built a family on mission with his disciples, how the early church continued to emulate what they learned from Jesus, and how the gospel spread through the family-on-mission structure of the *oikos* so every kind of person could be caught up in the story God was writing.

Whether you are single or married, have kids at home or don't, we all function best in the context of a family on mission. **So what does it look like to build family on mission today?** What are some footholds we could use to scale this mountain? What kind of equipment do we need? How do we begin? That's what rest of this book is all about. With the proper understanding and language to describe family on mission, we now can see from the life of Jesus and the early church how to participate in God's ongoing work by building and extending families on mission in our own lives.

THREE ESSENTIAL INGREDIENTS

Any family on mission rooted in Jesus will have his **shape**. The Russian mafia functions as a family on mission, but neither their mission vision nor their family values reflect the shape of Jesus' life very well, of course. If our family on mission is going to reflect the life of Jesus, what does it need to look like?

When we look at the life of Jesus, we notice that he lived a three-dimensional life, focusing on three great loves, three relational orientations: UP, IN, and OUT.

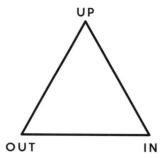

To say that Jesus lived UP means that he focused on his relationship with his Father. He was known for spending lots of time in prayer, and it was his regular habit to go to synagogue meetings and festivals in Jerusalem that were designed to help people connect with God. Jesus had a rich relationship with his Father—in other words, his life had an UP dimension.

Jesus also focused IN. Among the vast crowds that followed him, he chose twelve to be very close to him so he could train them and send them out. Jesus spent a lot of time with his disciples, so much so that they eventually became his family! He took them on retreat with him to invest time in them. By the end of his earthly ministry, their community was as tight-knit as they come. There was a strong IN dimension to Jesus' life.

JESUS' LIFE
was defined by missional purpose.

Of course, there was also a driving purpose to Jesus' life as he moved OUT. Mission defined his entire life and ministry. Just a few of the ways Jesus expressed this were "seeking and saving the lost," "destroying the works of the evil one," and "doing the will of him who sent me." Jesus' life was defined by missional purpose—his definitive OUT dimension.

The life of Jesus is a three-dimensional life, and so if our families are going to be shaped by Jesus they will also have this shape. There will be an UP aspect, an IN aspect, and an OUT aspect to the way we function as a family. As we look at what Jesus did in the Gospels, as well as how the early church emulated and multiplied that, we see three essential ingredients in building and multiplying a healthy family on mission. There needs to be

1. **Spiritual Parents (UP)**
2. **Predictable Patterns (IN)**
3. **Missional Purpose (OUT)**

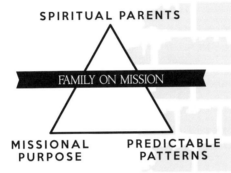

We'll talk about each one in much more detail below, but here are some brief explanations to begin to put some flesh on the bones.

SPIRITUAL PARENTS

Healthy families need parents, and healthy families on mission need **spiritual parents**. They don't need to be a married couple (Jesus was a single man, after all, but functioned as the spiritual parent of his family on mission), but someone (or ones) must take responsibility for the spiritual welfare and development of the family. This is what it means to be a spiritual parent.

Jesus functioned as the eldest brother and therefore "surrogate parent" of his disciples, revealing to them what the Father was like. He even called them his little children several times. The early church reflected this reality as well. Paul tells the Corinthians they have plenty of tutors but not enough fathers, and he urges them to imitate him, which is something a parent would encourage his or her child to do. The Apostle John writes to his disciples, calling them his dear children. Families on mission need spiritual parents.

PREDICTABLE PATTERNS

Healthy families need **predictable patterns** in order to thrive, and spiritual families are no different. A wealth of psychological research now supports this, but most importantly we see Jesus establishing predictable patterns with his disciples. Regular meals together, itinerant teaching, times of retreat and rest, routines of synagogue attendance and temple worship, and regular rhythms of personal prayer were just a few of the predictable patterns Jesus led his disciples in.

The early church picked up on this theme and the book of Acts reports that after the huge influx of believers on the day of Pentecost, they devoted themselves to the predictable patterns of the apostles' teaching, the breaking of bread, fellowship, and prayer. Families on mission need predictable patterns to help develop security in the family members' lives.

MISSIONAL PURPOSE

Healthy families need a sense of purpose greater than themselves. Families on mission by definition have a mission, which means they are reaching for a reality that transcends their own existence. Jesus obviously instilled a compelling sense of **missional purpose** in his family on mission. They didn't get together to hang out and have a good time—they were together to change the world, to see the kingdom of God advance, to see God's will done on earth as it is in heaven.

Their missional purpose was the driving force of their lives, the thing that compelled them to sacrifice and surrender their agendas for a greater good. Families on mission need missional purpose for their family to have a sense of movement forward.

TAKING STOCK

We'll be discussing each of these three elements in more detail in the coming chapters (including little triangles within the bit Family on Mission triangle!). But before we move on let's pause and think for a bit, because the Family on

Mission triangle is not just some interesting information. It's meant (like all of 3DM's tools) to function as a diagnostic tool that helps us observe where we're at and assess our current reality. If we take time to do this now, we'll have ears to hear the next few chapters, as we dive into the practicalities of growing in these three areas.

Right now, your family on mission may consist only of your nuclear family, or you and your roommates. (You may even be unsure of whether they are really with you on this journey.) Don't worry too much about this now. Simply think of those who are currently part of what you might call a spiritual family. Again, it could be your nuclear family at this point, but it could also include a larger extended *oikos*.

The Family on Mission triangle, like Jesus' parables, starts as a **picture**—a vision of reality, a truth to see and receive. But then it becomes a **mirror**—we see ourselves in it, and we're able to evaluate our own lives through it. But that's not the final stage. The last phase is when it becomes a **window**—we now see the world *through* the truth to which it points. In other words, it becomes a framework through which we see all of reality. It's how we go from simply having knowledge of facts to obtaining wisdom for life. We don't just *know* something new; we are able to *live* in a new way because we now see life through this window, which gives us access to more wisdom than we had before.

We've briefly discussed the tool as a picture of what a healthy family on mission looks like. It's the shape of a spiritual *oikos*, the goal we see in the life of Jesus for which we are aiming. So let's take a moment to use the Family on Mission triangle as a mirror, using it to look at our own lives before moving on to practical strategies for growth in these three areas. If these three components need to be in place for a healthy family on mission, how healthy is our family on mission right now?

SPIRITUAL PARENTS

FAMILY ON MISSION

MISSIONAL   PREDICTABLE
PURPOSE   PATTERNS

Think about being **spiritual parents**. How well are you calibrating this? Are you growing to be a spiritual parent who can have children who can reproduce themselves in the life of another? Are you able to offer your life as a living example of what it looks like to follow Jesus? Give yourself a score from 1 to 10, with 1 being "not very well at all," and 10 being "this is solidly in place."

Think about your **predictable patterns**. Are our rhythms as a family predictable or does life feel chaotic? Do I respond in predictable ways to those I am leading, or does my behavior change depending on my mood or circumstances? Again, give yourself a score from 1 to 10.

Finally, think about the **missional purpose** of your family/*oikos*. Is it clear? Does it looks like Jesus? Do the members of your family know what your purpose is? Is it reflected in the way you talk with one another and the way you spend your time? Give yourself a score from 1 to 10.

Take a look at your scores and perhaps share them with someone close to you. Notice what most grabs your attention.[13] Before moving on to the next chapters, spend some time in prayer, bringing whatever most stood out to you to the Lord, asking him "What do you want me to know about this?" Spend time listening, asking God to teach you about it.

---

[13] We call this a Kairos, and it's discussed in more detail in our book *Building a Discipling Culture*.

7

~ LEADING AS ~ SPIRITUAL PARENTS

DISCIPLESHIP AS PARENTING

Mike Writes:

Healthy families need parents, and spiritual families need spiritual parents— people who take responsibility to lead the family by laying down their lives and serving the family. Before we get into some practical examples of what this means, let's take a look at the biblical pattern on spiritual parenting and why this is the metaphor we use to discuss leading families on mission.

Jesus used his last words to commission his disciples to make more disciples, of all peoples, who would then make more disciples. The message was clear: to *be* a disciple meant that you learn how to *make* disciples— an ever-multiplying movement meant to bless the whole world. This would have been clearly understood in first-century Judaism. Everyone knew what a rabbi-disciple relationship looked like.

TO BE A DISCIPLE meant that you learn how to make disciples— an ever-multiplying movement meant to bless the whole world.

Throughout the Gospels and for most of the book of Acts, then, discipleship is the dominant metaphor for following Jesus. However, interestingly, after Acts 21, the word disciple disappears from the New Testament record. It isn't mentioned in any of Paul's, Peter's, or John's letters. All of them were trained as disciples, all of them trained their own disciples, and Jesus' last will and testament was to make disciples. So why don't they talk about discipleship in their letters?

Well, they do talk about discipleship after Acts 21—they just do it contextually; it's not a mistake that the word disappeared from the New Testament. We actually can learn quite a bit by tracing the language used here about discipleship and what it means to be a spiritual parent. Follow along for a bit and let me explain.

Here's Paul writing to the Corinthian church:

> I am writing this not to shame you but to warn you as my dear children. Even if you had ten thousand guardians in Christ, you do not have many fathers, for in Christ Jesus I became your father through the gospel. Therefore I urge you to imitate me. For this reason I have sent to you Timothy, my son whom I love, who is faithful in the Lord. He will remind you of my way of life in Christ Jesus, which agrees with what I teach everywhere in every church. [14]

It's clear from the other sources in the New Testament that Paul discipled Timothy, but in this passage Paul doesn't use that word. Peeling back some contextual layers in this passage begins to reveal clues that get us on the path to discover why discipleship disappears from the New Testament.

The word "guardian" is *pedagogos* in the original Greek. It essentially refers to a live-in tutor for children who was hired by a family and brought into their *oikos*. The *pedagogos* lived with the family and tutored the children in the basic information of a classical education: reading, writing, arithmetic, and logic.

When a child turned twelve, he or she went through a coming-of-age ritual, a moment of religious and societal significance in the *oikos* when children were handed from the *pedagogos* to their parents—the girls to their mothers and the boys to their fathers, to stand at their shoulders and learn the family business.

The mother of the *oikos* managed the whole household. She understood how to navigate the complexity of its relational and economic fabric. She knew how to deal with sickness in the *oikos*, oversaw the educational process, and managed the economic infrastructure and cash flow. She was the business manager and the shaper of a hospitable environment for guests.

---

[14] 1 Corinthians 4:14-17

The *pedagogos* would bring a twelve-year-old girl to her mother, and from that point on, the girl stood at the shoulder of her mother, basically walking beside her wherever she went, observing and learning through imitation how to manage the oikos in the way of her mother. A girl would discover how all the information she had learned from her *pedagogues* was lived out in everyday life. She walked wherever her mother walked, imitating her as her mother imitated her grandmother before her.

The process was the same for boys. They would stand at the shoulder of their father, going to every meeting, every jobsite, learning through imitation how to function in the family business, whether it was building or fishing or metalworking or farming.

So when Paul talks about the Corinthian believers having many "tutors" (*pedagogoi*) but not many fathers, he was referring to a pattern of life that everyone understood. They would have known he meant that there were lots of people around who could give them the right information, but what they truly needed to grow into the fullness of life in Christ was a father—a spiritual parent who would invite them into his or her life, giving access so they could imitate the way of Christ in the spiritual parent's life.

What is Paul doing here? It's important to remember that the gospel was moving away from its geographic and cultural genesis point of Judaism. The words written at the beginning of Acts are beginning to come true—the gospel is being preached not only in Jerusalem, Judea, and Samaria, but also now it's moving toward the "ends of the earth."

Corinth was similar to the majority of pagan cities in the ancient world. The people there had no understanding of what the word "disciple" meant or what it might mean to follow a rabbi because they didn't have rabbis and disciples. These people had no idea what a rabbi was or what a disciple looked like.

But the process of investment called "discipleship" still needed to be taught and modeled, so Paul looked for a comparison, a guiding picture that the fledgling church could understand that would lead them into the reality of following Jesus. He needed a picture that was similar enough to the full-orbed pattern of

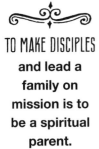

TO MAKE DISCIPLES
and lead a family on mission is to be a spiritual parent.

life that the rabbi-disciple relationship entailed without losing too much (or gaining too much) in translation. If you are being discipled by a rabbi, you certainly want to know what the rabbi knows. But the actual goal of being a disciple is to become who the rabbi is. Not just to know what he knows, but to become like him.

Paul understood this himself, but suddenly he was on mission to people who didn't have a cultural reference point for it. So he looked for an already-established cultural pattern that he could use to give them a picture of what it looked like to make disciples. As he observed their culture, the metaphor he settled on was **the parent and the child**.

He saw what happened when a child went from the tutelage of the *pedagogos* to the intense investment of standing at the shoulder of a parent, and he probably thought, "This is a great picture for it!" As children are raised, a *pedagogos* gives them necessary information that serves as a foundation for all their training in life, but the parent provides the model to imitate. Eventually those who imitate start households of their own and innovate on what they've learned, modeling for others what they themselves have learned.

This was the perfect metaphor for Paul, and thus, for the rest of the New Testament. The New Testament essentially replaces the rabbi-disciple relationship of the Gospels with the parent-child relationship of the epistles. Look at the rest of the New Testament. In almost every book, you see that the way the text understands the process of discipleship and spiritual formation is through the lens of parent and child.

Thus, to make disciples and lead a family on mission is to be a spiritual parent. Spiritual parents lead by example, give access to others to stand at your shoulder and imitate you as you imitate Christ, the model of what spiritual parenting is all about.

WHAT IT MEANS TO BE A PARENT

With Jesus as our model spiritual parent, we can look at his life and see what it means for us to grow as spiritual parents. Here's a framework we'll use to think about it. It's a little triangle within the big triangle of Family on Mission. It seems that being a spiritual parent means

- Cultivating **spiritual depth**
- **Submitting** to God, above your own agenda
- **Sacrificing** your personal desires for the good of the family you are leading

SPIRITUAL DEPTH

SPIRITUAL PARENTS

SACRIFICE   SUBMISSION

Let's take a look at how this is displayed in the life of Jesus and the early church.

JESUS AS SPIRITUAL PARENT

In the Gospels, we see Jesus acting as the spiritual parent for his disciples. As the eldest brother in the family, he is the "surrogate parent," which is what the eldest son would typically do if the father were traveling or otherwise unable to be personally present in the family. Jesus tells his disciples that he fully represents the Father to them, that he acts perfectly in alignment with his Father, and thus that when they are looking at him they are actually looking at the Father. He is the spiritual parent of their family on mission.

If you met Jesus and his twelve disciples and ate a meal with them, it wouldn't have been difficult to discern who the leader was. Jesus actually calls his disciples his "little ones."[15] People often think the passages where Jesus talks like this are about actual children, but Jesus clearly says that the "little ones" he is referring to are those who believe in him.

[15] Matthew 18:1-14

FOR JESUS, being a leader wasn't just about influencing people—it was about parenting children.

For Jesus, being a leader wasn't just about influencing people—it was about parenting children. It wasn't just a matter of trying to increase his reach—it was a matter of laying down his life for those he had taken responsibility for. Parenting is about love, which includes influence but encompasses much more. For the disciples, being with Jesus wasn't about hanging out with him. He wasn't their pal or work buddy. He was their rabbi, their master, their Lord. Jesus models spiritual depth, submission, and sacrifice perfectly for his disciples.

SPIRITUAL DEPTH

More than anyone else, Jesus had **spiritual depth**. He knew the source of his ability to minister effectively was the quality of his relationship with his Father. This is why he often rose early to pray, even after a late evening of ministry. He knew the secret of his power was that the Father was in him, and he was in the Father. This is the relationship he invited the disciples to share as they began to invest in others, becoming spiritual parents themselves.

Spiritual parents operate from their spiritual depth. Jesus makes it clear that they cannot simply be people with a lot of natural leadership skill, or charisma, or influence, or gravitas. They must be people who are intimately connected to God, like a branch is connected to a vine—constantly dwelling in the nourishing relationship that allows the branch to bear fruit.[16] Spiritual parents are people who are growing ever deeper in their walk with God.

If you're going to be a spiritual parent, you need spiritual resources, and Jesus showed us that the only place to get them is from God. You parent others spiritually out of your relationship with God. There is no other source from which to draw that empowers you to do it. Draw on your relationship with God for the resources you need to parent those who are following you. Share with them out of the overflow of what God is doing in your own life.

. . . .

[16] John 15:1-8

SUBMISSION

Jesus modeled **submission** as well. Spiritual parents who carry authority are those who are submitted to authority. Jesus did not operate independently. He laid aside the independent use of his divine attributes and submitted himself to operating as a human being to show us the way. Jesus said he did only what he saw the Father doing. He was radically submitted to the Father's agenda, and followed through with it even to the point of cruel torture and death on a Roman cross. "Not my will, but yours be done" is the prayer of a spiritual parent who is submitted to *his* Parent.

As we see in Jesus, being submitted means that we are prepared to set aside our own agendas for the greater good. It means we are able to set aside our own personal desires and ambitions for the purposes of the blessing and growth of the group that we're called to lead.

However, being submissive doesn't mean that we never share our opinions and feelings about things. Even Jesus, before he committed himself to the Father's will in Gethsemane, spoke about his desires and concerns: "My Father, if it is possible, may this cup be taken from me. Yet not as I will, but as you will."[17] A truly submitted person may give all kinds of reasons why he doesn't want to do something, or why she thinks it's a bad idea. Far from people who just "drank the Kool-Aid" or shut down their hearts, they'll speak honestly about what they think of something but then still submit to their Father. Those are truly submissive people.

Jesus told a parable about a man who had two sons.[18] He told the first to go and work in the vineyard. "I will not!" the first son said, but later changed his mind and worked. The man told his second son to go and work in the vineyard, to which he replied, "I will, sir!" but then never went. Jesus' point was that the first son did the will of his father, despite his protests. That's what it means to truly submit. It means you share freely what you think about things, but at the end of the day, do

> **BEING SUBMITTED means that we are prepared to set aside our own agendas for the greater good.**

---

[17] Matthew 26:39

[18] Matthew 21:28-32

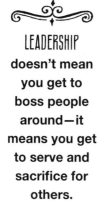

LEADERSHIP doesn't mean you get to boss people around—it means you get to serve and sacrifice for others.

it anyway. The non-submissive person is the one who stays silent, pretending or even intending to do what has been asked of him, but never actually doing it.

Spiritual parents need to imitate Jesus in his submission to the Father's authority.

SACRIFICE

Finally, Jesus demonstrates and teaches his disciples what it means to **sacrifice** as a spiritual parent. Perhaps there is no better encapsulation of this than a conversation Jesus has with his disciples at their last supper together before his crucifixion. In the midst of the intimacy and gravity of that moment, "a dispute arose among them as to which of them was considered to be greatest."[19] Nothing like an old-fashioned chest-thumping contest to ruin an important moment! Jesus takes it in stride, though, and uses it as an opportunity to talk with them about the true nature of leadership in his kingdom. He says to them,

> The kings of the Gentiles lord it over them; and those who exercise authority over them call themselves Benefactors. But you are not to be like that. Instead, the greatest among you should be like the youngest, and the one who rules like the one who serves. For who is greater, the one who is at the table or the one who serves? Is it not the one who is at the table? But I am among you as one who serves.[20]

The youngest person in the family was the one who got the most menial and unflattering jobs. Jesus was telling them that their measurement of what it meant to lead and be great wasn't calibrated correctly for his kingdom. Instead, being great meant you were like the youngest in the family, unashamed to do the most menial of jobs, like washing the dust and dung off the feet of those gathered for supper. Leadership doesn't mean you get to boss people around—it means you get to serve and sacrifice for others. Jesus pointed to

....

[19] Luke 22:24
[20] Luke 22:25-27

his own life as an example of how to lead, how to be a spiritual parent.

As spiritual parents, we are called to sacrifice for those we are leading. Would the people we lead say that we serve them? Or would they say that they serve us? You might even ask some of them, if you're feeling especially daring. That's the basic question: Do we serve people or use them? Empower them or overpower them? Control and dominate or serve and help flourish? Spiritual parents lay down their lives for those they lead—they give blood, sweat, and tears in the midst of a relationship, not just advice and technique from a distance.

A VIVID PICTURE OF LEADERSHIP

This picture of spiritual parenting is driven home in a metaphor that Jesus gives us at the end of John's Gospel, after his resurrection when he reinstates Peter (who had betrayed Jesus at the crucifixion). It's a vivid picture of what it means to be a spiritual parent. Peter, likely depressed about his failure on the night of Jesus' crucifixion, takes a few other disciples and goes back to fishing—the family business of his old *oikos*. They fish all night without success, and then see a stranger on the shore who urges them to try throwing their nets on the other side of the boat. They gather a miraculously large catch of fish that threatens to swamp their boats, and Peter suddenly recognizes that it's Jesus on the beach. In typical Peter fashion, he jumps in the water with all his clothes on and swims for shore.

When Peter arrives on the beach, wet and cold, he sees that Jesus has a charcoal fire burning, and is cooking fish and bread for breakfast. Perhaps Peter remembered another charcoal fire at which he warmed his hands only a few days earlier, when he vehemently denied that he knew Jesus. Perhaps he felt sick to his stomach because he wasn't sure how Jesus was going to respond.

Jesus calmly tells Peter to go get some of the fish he had just caught, and tells the disciples to come and have breakfast. After they had breakfast, Jesus doesn't scold or lecture Peter—he simply asks Peter three times, "Do you love me?" Peter answers each time in the affirmative, and when he does, Jesus calls him into the role of a shepherd: "Feed my lambs." "Take care of my sheep." "Feed my sheep." These are the specific tasks of a shepherd.

Peter's reinstatement metaphor is that of **shepherd**.

What's interesting about this is that of all the pictures of leadership in the New Testament, shepherd is probably the one with the least status in the minds of the people of the time. Shepherds were not held in high regard. The picture of a shepherd is the picture of the youngest in the family doing the most menial job. The youngest in the family has the lowest status, and therefore gets the lowest job anyone could think of: shepherd.

Think of David out in the fields watching his father's sheep. He was the youngest son of Jesse with so little status that when Samuel the prophet stops by and asks to see Jesse's sons, no one even thinks of going to fetch David. Can you imagine? This is probably the only time any of these people will ever meet the most famous man in Israel, and David wouldn't have even heard about it if Samuel hadn't insisted they go get him from the fields. No position. No status. That's what a shepherd is.

Our word "pastor" comes from the biblical word for shepherd, and today we think of pastor as the highest position in a church. But it wouldn't have sounded like that to Peter. Imagine telling a leader the metaphor that will help him understand his leadership is intern or errand boy. I'm sure Peter's chest didn't puff up with pride at hearing Jesus' words around that fire.

What Jesus is doing here is reinstating Peter, but not as the firstborn son of the household who will represent the father in all matters. Instead, Jesus reinstates Peter as the youngest son, testing his heart to see whether he will receive shepherd as his portfolio of leadership. Will you do the most menial task? Will you simply serve the people I love, even if you aren't honored for it? Jesus wants to know if Peter will do the most menial task out of love, or if he will be offended by the suggestion that he should do something as lowly as shepherding.

IMAGINE TELLING **a leader the metaphor that will help them understand their leadership is intern or errand boy.**

This becomes one of the most common metaphors for leadership in the New Testament. Being a shepherd is a picture of what it means to be a spiritual parent. Later, Peter uses this metaphor to write to the elders of the church, the old ones in the *oikoses*, to encourage them to function like Jesus as spiritual parents.

*To the elders among you, I appeal as a fellow elder and a witness
of Christ's sufferings who also will share in the glory to be revealed:
Be shepherds of God's flock that is under your care, watching over
them--not because you must, but because you are willing, as God
wants you to be; not pursuing dishonest gain, but eager to serve;
not lording it over those entrusted to you, but being examples to the
flock. And when the Chief Shepherd appears, you will receive the
crown of glory that will never fade away.*

*In the same way, you who are younger, submit yourselves to your
elders. All of you, clothe yourselves with humility toward one
another, because,*

"God opposes the proud but shows favor to the humble."

*Humble yourselves, therefore, under God's mighty hand, that he
may lift you up in due time. Cast all your anxiety on him because
he cares for you. Be alert and of sober mind. Your enemy the devil
prowls around like a roaring lion looking for someone to devour.
Resist him, standing firm in the faith, because you know that the
family of believers throughout the world is undergoing the same kind
of sufferings.*

*And the God of all grace, who called you to his eternal glory in
Christ, after you have suffered a little while, will himself restore you
and make you strong, firm and steadfast. To him be the power for
ever and ever. Amen.*[21]

Peter is speaking to spiritual parents here, people who function as overseers
in the New Testament *oikos*. He tells the spiritual parents in each spiritual
household that they should function as shepherds, who, like Jesus the good
shepherd, live in a different way toward others than most expect a leader to
live. A good shepherd lays down her life for the sheep, isn't greedy for money,
isn't looking for prominence, and isn't lording her leadership over people.

In other words, Peter is saying that, according to Jesus, being a spiritual
parent involves becoming the kind of person who serves others instead of

---

[21] 1 Peter 5:1-11

BEING A SPIRITUAL parent involves becoming the kind of person who serves others instead of themselves.

themselves, a person who can submit to others, humble and eager to serve, the kind of person who has enough spiritual depth to carry the weight of being a spiritual parent, aware that the devil is prowling around, looking for someone to devour, and that the Lord is very near, so they can cast all of their anxieties and burdens on the Lord.

We see the early church emulating this method of leadership. The Apostle John writes to his "dear children." The Apostle Paul casts himself in the role of a father to the Corinthian church, and like any good father in those days, urges them to imitate him. Paul even refers to himself as a "nursing mother" to the Thessalonian believers, loving and sharing his life with them.[22] It's a very tender picture of what it really feels like to enter into this kind of relationship with others. Being a leader in the early church meant being a spiritual parent to those who were following you, which meant taking responsibility for the welfare of your children. You lay down your life for them. You sacrifice for them.

---

[22] 1 Thessalonians 2:7-8

WHERE IT LEADS

Sally Writes:

As you parent in this way, cultivating spiritual depth, submitting your agenda to the greater good, and sacrificing on behalf of those you're leading in your family on mission, where does it all lead? Do these people stay at your house forever? Are they always spiritual children?

Thinking about what happens in a normal family is a helpful lens. Often, people within the extended family want to form their own family. This is good and healthy. They grow up and become mature and are able to establish their own household and possibly move away. But the relationship remains. It just looks a little different. There are still regular phone calls, predictable contact, and they often return for the festivals—birthdays, Thanksgiving, Christmas, that sort of thing. Their orbit becomes wider because they have begun to establish an orbit around themselves!

In our lives, Jo and Chris Saxton are great examples of this. Jo started hanging around our family in England when she was single. She would join us for meals and help the kids with their homework. She was around a lot! Eventually, she got married to Chris and obviously came around less. (We'd have been worried if she didn't!) Chris and Jo were building their own household.

In time, they then moved with us to Phoenix and had their own biological children. During this period, they had dinner with us once a week and spent holidays with us, but we didn't have as much time together because they had their own children (both biological and spiritual) to invest in.

Now we live hundreds of miles away from each other, but we still talk and text often. They have lots of young adults in their own *oikos* where they live, but we hold the same vision and values, because we come from the same extended family. We see each other for various

JUST AS KIDS grow up and move out and reproduce, spiritual children ought to grow up to become spiritual parents.

3DM events and try to get together and celebrate once a year.

Just as kids grow up and move out and reproduce, spiritual children ought to grow up to become spiritual parents, starting their own spiritual families.

GETTING STARTED

I encourage you to look at your life right now and think, "Am I called to be a spiritual parent in this season, leading a family on mission? Or am I called in this season to be part of someone else's family on mission?"

It's a really important question, because it defines how you relate in the family on mission you're part of. Obviously not everyone in the family on mission can be spiritual parents! Being the spiritual parents isn't better or worse than being the spiritual children, but it's important to have clarity about it.

For example, many of the people who moved down to Pawleys Island to join our family on mission came from situations where they were the spiritual parents of their own families on mission, but sensed God leading them into a season where they would join our family on mission. And many of the people who have joined us here are now starting Missional Communities, which are the seedbeds of them starting their own families on mission inside our big family on mission!

One way to think about this is to simply look around and see if people are orienting themselves toward you. Are there people around you who seem to want to hang out with you? People who ask you a lot of questions? People who like you, listen to you, and serve you? You may be called to act as a spiritual parent in that person's life.

Try making a list of people who seem to be orienting themselves toward you, and then rank them in how "close" they are. Are they functioning as friends? Are they followers? Are they family? This is a good way to at least begin thinking about what it would mean for you to become a spiritual parent.

8

～ GROWING IN ～ PREDICTABLE PATTERNS

WHY PREDICATABLE PATTERNS?

Mike Writes:

One year, Sally and I decided we were going to get a puppy for the children for Christmas. I had found out about a local woman named Mrs. Hopkinson who was a famous breeder of Labradors, and I went to see her and get one of her new puppies. I assumed it would be a simple transaction, but when I arrived, I found out that I wasn't just buying a puppy—I was being interviewed for the job of caring for one of Mrs. Hopkinson's puppies. She wanted to find out whether *I* was a suitable candidate for one of her dogs.

She asked me all kinds of questions about how I planned to care for the puppy and told me what kind of environment the puppy needed. Will someone be around the house all the time? Will there be adequate exercise and nutrition and interaction? Thankfully, I passed Mrs. Hopkinson's exam, and we were cleared to pick up the puppy for the children around Christmastime. We were going to name her Holly.

When it got closer to Christmas, Mrs. Hopkinson laid out an elaborate plan for how to pick up Holly. There were specific instructions on whom she should meet first, how to give Holly her first meal, how to introduce her to the other members of the family, what to do in the first few days at home, and more. It struck me as a little over the top, but Mrs. Hopkinson told me, "Mr. Breen, if you don't give her a framework, she'll never be happy."

We did as Mrs. Hopkinson said, and I'm glad we did, because while Holly wasn't a perfect dog (she would occasionally raid the neighbor's trashcans), she was an absolutely delightful pet that loved taking her place in our family and that always obeyed when we gave her instructions. She seemed like a happy dog, just as Mrs. Hopkinson predicted. The predictable framework we provided produced a secure, content, and happy dog.

People aren't dogs, of course, but the same principle applies to our families on mission. Cornel West once said that "justice is what love looks like in public." I love that, and I'd take it further to say that **predictable patterns** are what love looks like in a family. Just as justice is the key to society flourishing, so too predictable patterns are the key to the flourishing of our family on mission. They are one of the primary ways spiritual parents set their spiritual children up to succeed and find significance.

In a culture that values novelty and spontaneity, it is fashionable to view predictability as a bit boring—not as exciting as mission seems like it should be. So let's ask: Why are we so keen on predictable patterns? Where do we see this in Scripture? And why is it important? Why not spontaneous new stuff all the time? What about predictable patterns creates family on mission?

First, we see it in the way Jesus parented his family on mission. He established predictable patterns with his disciples in the regular meals they eat together, his itinerant teaching, times of retreat and rest, routines of synagogue attendance and temple worship, and regular rhythms of personal prayer. Certainly there were times when these rhythms were interrupted or had to be shelved for a season, but the general pattern seems to be that Jesus established predictable patterns for the disciples.

PREDICTABLE PATTERNS
are what love looks like in a family.

In addition to their rhythm of life, there was predictability about the way Jesus responded to situations and people. There wasn't a sense of insecurity when someone approached him or began to argue with him or tried to refute him. People weren't unsure about he would respond. He remained very predictable in his responses to the disciples, the Pharisees, and the crowds.

The early church picked up on this theme. The book of

Acts reports that after the huge influx of believers on the day of Pentecost, they devoted themselves to the predictable patterns of the apostles' teaching, the breaking of bread, fellowship, and prayer. These were commitments they made, not just events they attended if they didn't have anything else going on. It was a discipline, a rhythm for them. The predictable pattern allowed them to grow more deeply into faith.

A wealth of psychological research out now indicates that predictable patterns are important for every child's development.[23] We believe spiritual children are no different.

STABILITY

Predictable patterns mean that the most important things are done intentionally and consistently. This brings **stability** to the family. The rhythm of knowing what's coming brings peace and comfort to the life of any family. It's not that every minute of every day is scheduled. We are simply building regular rhythms into our days, weeks, and months that create fixed points of reference around which the family can orient itself.

Predictable patterns are the fixed points of reference we put into our schedule to make sure we are actually practicing the most important things in life. I can't expect my kids to value prayer and time in the Bible if we haven't done that together each day as a family. I can't expect my kids to value deep relationships unless we have regular times, like meals, where we gather together to pay attention to one another and share our lives with each other.

Making these patterns regular and predictable, as opposed to sporadic and spontaneous, is what gives children (as well as anyone who is part of our extended family on mission) a sense of stability in their lives. It's remarkable how true this is for our biological children and the "spiritual children" we are investing in as spiritual parents.

....

[23] Just search the Internet for "routines and child development" for a start. Dr. Peter Gorski, assistant professor of pediatrics at Harvard Medical School, says this, "Knowing what to expect from relationships and activities helps children become more confident."

SECURITY

Embracing predictable patterns over time builds stability, and when stability is experienced over time, it creates **security** for the members of a family. They become secure in their identity, which then becomes an unshakable foundation they carry with them wherever they go. People who are secure in their identity can become spiritual parents and make disciples. People who aren't secure in their identity can't. Helping our children, spiritual and biological, experience security is extremely important, because it's the foundation on which everything else is built.

In the same way that Jesus' identity was affirmed and solidified before he began his mission, we need all our missional activity to be rooted firmly in a secure identity in a family. Our families need the stability that comes from predictable patterns of UP, IN, and OUT. Those patterns give us security in our identity, so we know who we are and why we exist as a family. Covenantal identity and security is the root from which the tree of kingdom mission grows.

SIGNIFICANCE

What does operating out of a secure identity produce? The ability to live a life of **significance**. Significance is not necessarily the same thing as success. There are no guarantees about how successful we'll be. Those kinds of outcomes are in the Lord's hands. But we know that if we engage in our work from a place of security in our identity, our work will be significant, meaning that it is being used by God to advance his kingdom, whether anyone knows about it or not.

> **WHEN STABILITY** is experienced over time it creates security for the members of a family.

Jesus was always going about his Father's business, which meant it was always significant, whether he was being followed by adoring crowds or being threatened with death by those same crowds, whether he was preaching to thousands or praying with a few friends in a garden, whether people were amazed at his teaching or appalled at his crucifixion. It was all significant, because it came from a secure identity.

A life of significance comes a secure identity born in a family of stability, cultivated in predictable patterns.

That's why these things are the key to helping our children (or anyone who is part of our extended family on mission!) live into a life of significance.

WHAT KINDS OF PATTERNS?

So what kinds of patterns do we need to be predictable about?

As Sally and I have looked at what Jesus did for his disciples and tried to imitate that in our own *oikos*, we have boiled predictable patterns down to three things, another little triangle within the big triangle of Family on Mission. Predictable patterns involve these three things:

- **Love**
- **Discipline**
- **Freedom**

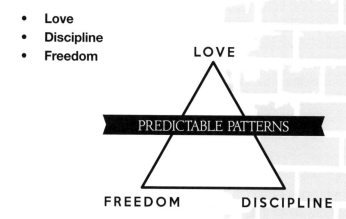

These aren't three different things to do a different times—they are elements of an integrated whole. Love, for example, isn't something different from discipline. In a spiritual family on mission, love is expressed to children through discipline and freedom. Sally and I tend to complement each other in this regard. I was raised in a military home, potty-trained at gunpoint (not really), which has led to a slightly uptight personality. So my tendency is to express my love first through discipline. Sally, on the other hand, was raised in a bohemian, barefoot hippie family with flowers in her hair, and she tends to first express love by giving freedom. She helps me with the freedom part, and I help her with the discipline part. It's often like that in marriage.

As we've helped each other, we've been more able to create a culture of unconditional love through the predictable patterns of discipline and freedom. Let's take a look at what each element entails.

WHAT LOVE LOOKS LIKE

Sally Writes:

Love is one of those things that's easy to grasp conceptually, but sometimes difficult to implement practically. I mean, we'd all say that we love our children, wouldn't we? And of course that's true. But what does love look like? What does love do on a Thursday? How can we help our children *feel* more unconditionally loved?

The goal we have as parents is to unconditionally love our children, biological and spiritual. This means we tell them we love them and that we are pleased with them, just as the Father spoke words of love and affirmation to Jesus at his baptism. We tell them that we're proud of them. We tell them our love for them will never change, no matter how they behave. We want to model God's love in our love for them. If our love is conditional on their attitude or behavior, it's not the same kind of love that God has for us.

That means that no matter what they've done, they need to be able to rest in the confidence that our love for them does not change. This of course gives them a concrete picture of what it means when we tell them that God loves them. We don't do it perfectly of course, but it's important for children to experience unconditional love as a bedrock foundation for everything else in life. This means we have to express that love to them in words and action, often.

THE GOAL
we have as parents is to unconditionally love our children, biological and spiritual.

It's important to be constant, unchanging, and vocal in our love for one another, just as we are with our biological children. We continually have to repeat: we don't love you for what you do, but for who you are. We try to do exactly the same for our extended spiritual family, giving public praise but private discipline.

An example or two from our biological family may help to shed light on what this could look like in a spiritual family. One of the ways Mike and I tried to be intentional with unconditional love was to spend time looking and talking with our children about their weaknesses. It's easy for children to feel loved when we praise them for something they are good at, but if that's the only time they experience love from us, we may be sending them a subtle but powerful message that they experience love only when they perform well.

We wanted our children to experience love in the midst of failure and weakness, so we made it a normal practice to talk with them about their failures and weaknesses, the things they weren't good at and needed to grow in. It wasn't scolding; it was simply an expression of love to kindly point out areas of struggle for them. The result was that they became very secure and able to receive challenge, because they knew they were loved even when being challenged. Their weaknesses didn't come as a surprise to them in their teenage years, because it was just a normal thing to talk about in the context of love.

So everyone in our family knew that Libby was the one who was going to slam doors and have a tendency to let her anger run away with her. We all knew that Beccy was the one who was going to cry in the corner and not want to get out of bed. We all knew each other's weaknesses and tendencies, but simply loved one another in the midst of it. Everyone knew that they were loved even in the midst of their failures. At least that was our goal. We didn't always get it right, of course, but it's amazing how much grace there is when you simply make a choice to unconditionally love your children for who they actually are, not who you want them to be.

When we did get it wrong, we simply apologized to our children. This is a really important thing for parents to do. This further reinforced the idea that our family was a safe place to fail. It was a safe place to be weak, because even Mom and Dad get it wrong sometimes, and they apologize for it when the do. It becomes a community where we all know we are living with weakness, and it allows us to give each other grace and extend forgiveness liberally. It just makes life work.

WHAT DISCIPLINE LOOKS LIKE

Mike Writes:

It's sometimes difficult to tell this nowadays, with the emergence of helicopter parenting, but the role of parents is to raise adults who are good people rather than trying to make sure our kids always like us and become our friends. If you raise your kids to be good people, there will be a strong possibility they will be friends with you when they grow up, but this cannot be your goal. If your goal in parenting is for your kids to like you, you'll never be able to give them the kind of investment they need to become mature adults. To invest in your children in a way that brings them to maturity, you need to be able to bring them both invitation and challenge, and you can't challenge people if you need them to like you.

Again, using some illustrations from our biological family will help us move toward thinking about spiritual families on mission. What we sought to do for our children was to establish discipline that positively reinforced behavior that was unselfish, considerate, and helpful to others. So we met twice a day for meals as a family: breakfast and dinner. It didn't matter what you were involved in or how tired you were, you needed to show up at breakfast and dinner. We didn't allow individual preference to define how we lived together. Sometimes that meant we had breakfast really early in the morning if I was leaving for a trip. Sometimes it meant you couldn't go out with your friends until after dinner.

Breakfast and dinner were times of re-connection and value-strengthening. We prayed together, ate together, discussed together. Pretty much every day. It was a discipline that reinforced our value of community instead of individualism.

Another discipline we engaged in regularly was something we called Appreciation Dinner. It worked like this: at dinner everyone would share one thing he or she appreciated about every other person. Everyone shared several things they appreciated, and everyone got appreciated several times. Sometimes we'd have to encourage someone to dig a little deeper and not just say the same thing they said last time, but overall it was awesome! There were smiles all around the table, because it feels good to be appreciated, and feels even better to appreciate others. Everybody won at Appreciation Dinner. Again, this was a discipline we engaged in that reinforced the kind of attitude we wanted our kids to grow up with: one that actively appreciates and encourages others. It was a way of discipling them into unselfish ways of living.

Another regular pattern was called Daddy's Breakfast, where one of the kids would go out for breakfast with me on Saturday morning. They got to choose where we ate breakfast and what we did. When they were younger, it was McDonald's. When they got older, it was places called Cafe Rouge where we drank tea and read sophisticated newspapers. It was a discipline that taught the children that their opinions and desires were legitimate, and that we were interested in their lives.

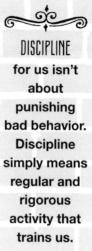

DISCIPLINE for us isn't about punishing bad behavior. Discipline simply means regular and rigorous activity that trains us.

DISCIPLINE VS PUNISHMENT

You'll notice that discipline for us isn't about punishing bad behavior. Discipline simply means regular and rigorous activity that trains us. That's what breakfast and dinner were about. Discipline is really about creating a framework that keeps returning us to who God is and who we are. You could think about discipline as a framework that helps us remember who we are. Punishment is about behavior, but discipline is about identity.

Deb Sternke, who is part of the 3DM team, recently came up with a chart that helps parents distinguish between punishment and discipline.

PUNISHMENT	DISCIPLINE
Focus on past misdeeds	Focus on future good works
Repayment & getting what you deserve	Guidance & getting what you need
Guilt, fear, shame	Security, love, support
Disempowering	Empowering
Behavior-focused	Identity-focused
Inflicting penalty for offense	Training for godliness and maturity
Suffering for wrong-doing	Appropriate consequences for learning

Of course, sometimes we needed to confront behavior that didn't line up with our values, but it was always very important for us to distinguish between childish foolishness (which is to be expected) and rebellion (which is something entirely different). We always disciplined attitude (not just behavior) if it was selfish or individualistic, because the ability to sacrifice and submit are life skills that you can learn, rather than personality traits.

Foolishness or irresponsibility was met with simple correction, such as a new boundary or a conversation. Rebellion (things like deception and willful disobedience) were met with the revocation of privilege. The message was that these kinds of things are out-of-bounds in a covenant relationship like family.

PATTERNS THAT BUILD CONFIDENCE

There were all kinds of other predictable patterns of discipline. Sometimes they shifted and changed based on how old the kids were and what their current needs were. If one of the kids had a rough day at school, we'd get out the Special Plate to comfort and encourage them. We had routines for the morning and for bedtime. We had family rituals for Christmas and Easter and birthdays. We had family OUT days when we'd do mission together. The kids would come on ministry trips with me to see how Jesus was doing amazing things in other parts of the world, too.

There were certain non-negotiables, like making your bed and opening the curtains in the morning, no TVs in their rooms, no sitting alone in their rooms with the door closed for hours, breakfast and dinner. You'll have to decide what those regular patterns of discipline will be for your family, but remember they're all meant to be expressions of love for your family on mission.

WITH THIS KIND of discipline anyone who is raised within its framework becomes confident instead of fearful.

Sally says discipline helps us set the bar high for our children. We did expect a lot from our children, and today we expect a lot from those who are part of our family on mission in Pawleys Island. We don't expect perfect performance, but we expect a lot in terms of conduct and character. What we find is that when we expect these things, people tend to grow into it. What happens with this kind of discipline is that anyone who is raised within its framework becomes confident instead of fearful. Punishment produces fear and insecurity, but discipline produces confidence and security. That's exactly what people need if they're going to lean into freedom.

WHAT FREEDOM LOOKS LIKE

Along with discipline, **freedom** is the other way that love is expressed in a family on mission. Here's what we believe: a moderately disciplined life lets you soar. We need to give our spiritual children permission and empowerment to soar, to explore, to try things. Jesus was constantly giving his disciples way more freedom than they were comfortable with, seeing what they'd do with it, curious how they'd manage it. He sent them out two by two to try the things he'd been doing himself up until that point. When they returned, he was overjoyed that their adventure had borne good fruit. They had gone out in freedom, and then returned to the framework of their predictable patterns together.

With our own family, when our kids were growing up we established a framework through the disciplines we just talked about, and then encouraged our kids to explore with freedom. Have fun. Express yourself as an individual creatively and artistically. Try new things, whether you succeed or fail. A family on mission needs to have an environment where it's OK to try things out before we know if we're good at them or not. There needs to be an ability to tell some jokes, lighten up and laugh a bit. One of the ways our own children experienced freedom was that we were constantly playing (light-hearted) practical jokes on one another.

Freedom is the other side of discipline, and typically people do not feel loved if you have one without the other. Freedom without discipline feels like chaos, and some of the most stifling environments are those where there is freedom without a framework of discipline. Likewise, discipline without freedom feels constricting, and will likely lead to rebellion once a child gets frustrated enough with the lack of freedom. In both cases, the result is fear. If everything is disciplined and controlled, people will become fearful, but they'll also become fearful if there is no framework. Freedom and discipline work together to create spiritual children who are confident and secure.

CELL PHONE FREEDOM

Sally Writes:

Here's an example of freedom within a framework. We gave our children mobile phones when they were quite young. They got them before most of their friends did. The reason we did this was so that they'd have a way of speaking with Mike when he was traveling. This was an expression of freedom that we allowed them, but we gave them a framework for using the phones. We simply told them they needed to engage in a self-imposed discipline of not chatting for hours on it (we didn't have texting and video chatting back then, so I suppose you'll need different kinds of frameworks today). The consequence for abusing the privilege was simply the confiscation of the phone. I can't think of a time they ever abused it. The freedom it gave them was a blessing to them because it was given within a framework of discipline.

CHASING BUTTERFLIES

Mike Writes:

There's an anecdote I heard a long time ago that brilliantly illustrates how freedom and discipline work together. A toddler and her mother are at a park, sitting on a bench together. As the toddler begins to play, she sees a beautiful monarch butterfly fluttering a few feet away. She looks at her mother, then back at the butterfly, plucks up enough courage and begins toddling toward the butterfly, giggling and reaching out her hands. Suddenly she feels a little insecure because she has wandered several feet away from her mother, so she toddles back to her mother and touches her. Her mother says, "I love you, sweetie. Are you chasing a butterfly? That's wonderful!" As she receives value and love from her mother, her little tank of courage gets filled back up, and she toddles off again to chase the butterfly.

In this story, freedom is the toddler chasing the butterfly, letting go of Mom and exploring something she has an interest in. Discipline is simply the connecting point when she returns to her mother to touch base. That's what discipline does—creates a framework within which people can touch base and connect. Discipline is about connection.

DISCIPLINE is about connection.

That's why eating breakfast together every day is a good discipline. It helps you to connect as a family. It's also a discipline to *not* go to your room and shut the door when you're frustrated with the rest of the family. It's a good discipline because it helps you connect. (That was a rule in our house, by the way. We had to work it out instead of isolate ourselves.) Disciplines are about connection. Freedom is about exploration. Recognize that you probably have a tendency to lean one way or another, and make sure you are intentional about your spiritual children having both.

PREDICTABLE PATTERNS TODAY

Sally Writes:

Even though our children are grown now, we still live our lives by predictable patterns. We just do it now with our big extended spiritual family in Pawleys Island—our *oikos*. Of course the patterns are different now, because we're in a different stage. We don't have children living in our home (except when our grandson spends the night), we have lots of young families who have moved here to be on mission with us, so we continue to have predictable patterns that allow us to function together as a family on mission.

For example, every morning Monday through Friday, we spend thirty minutes worshiping, praying, and reading Scripture. It is a predictable pattern, and we often have visitors who come and join us from the surrounding community. Nobody wonders if that will be happening—you can predict it will happen because it's our regular pattern. We typically have twenty or more people in the room now, but we practiced this predictable pattern years ago when it was just a few of us.

Every Sunday evening we gather at 6 PM for a more extended time of worship and word. Many from the surrounding community join us for this as well. It's a predictable pattern that implants security in our family on mission.

Even little things make a difference. You can predict that Mike will be watching a movie on Friday night and watching soccer on Saturday morning. You can predict that I will find a way to go to Starbucks on the weekend. You can predict that our *oikos* will gather at the beach at least once a month. You know what to expect when you come into our home.

> **WE CONTINUE to have predictable patterns that allow us to function together as a family on mission.**

So if you're running a Missional Community, it's probably really helpful to have the mugs in the same place every time, the same rules about the toys in the basement, the same location and rules for the food, the same location for the coats, etc. Try as much as possible to do the same things every time.

When we host 3DM Learning Community dinners in our home, for example, people can typically predict that we will spend some time eating together, and later we might go out onto the deck to sit by the fire. If you're part of the 3DM family, you know you're expected to be warm and hospitable to the guests, and help out with the setting up and cleaning up.

Predictable patterns just help people feel confident because they aren't stressed about what might happen. They know what's happening and what's expected, and how to be part of what's going on. Many on our team try to stay connected to their family's predictable patterns through technology. Video chatting is a wonderful way to stay plugged into a predictable pattern with your family when you have to travel. Many on our team join their families for breakfast even when they're on the road, just by setting up an iPad on the breakfast table. It makes a big difference in how the children experience their parents traveling.

Finally, it's worth noting that all of this is basically hard work. It's actually not complicated; it's just hard work to stay consistent even when you feel like you want to take a break. Stick with it, because the product you get at the end of it is worth it! A family on mission that has security in their identity is a force to be reckoned with.

GETTING STARTED

It can feel overwhelming to see all the examples of predictable patterns and think that somehow you are supposed to implement all of them at once. Thankfully, this is not true (or possible). What I encourage you to do is simply pick one new predictable pattern that you'd like to implement, and do that. Be intentional about it, cast vision to the others in your family on mission about it— tell them why you're doing something new and what you hope it will achieve.

Just focus on getting that one new habit implemented. You'll miss some days and forget other days. Don't worry about it, don't beat yourself up over it, just start over the next day. Be as consistent as you can be, even if it's difficult at first. Just do this one thing until it starts to become part of the fabric of your life, and then try moving on to another predictable pattern and do it again!

It's amazing how powerful a simple predictable pattern is. One of the families at 3DM has been doing family breakfast for about a year now. They have a very simple rhythm: while eating together, they do three things within the span of about 10 minutes:

1. They share what they are thankful and hopeful for today.
2. They read a portion of Scripture together.
3. They pray together for the day and any needs.

They've been practicing this for a year or so. One recent morning, both Mom and Dad were sick and unable to be at breakfast as usual. To their delight, they heard their kids leading family breakfast by themselves! One child led the time of sharing thankful and hopeful, another read Scripture from their devotional book, and a third led the family in prayer. Then they went off to school! Predictable patterns are powerful in shaping the culture of a family on mission.

9

∾ MOVING OUT ∾ IN MISSIONAL PURPOSE

THE MISSION IS JESUS

Mike Writes:

Spiritual parents who set up predictable patterns for a family on mission to live by. However, ultimately, the reason the family exists has to be defined by **missional purpose**. Mission is the integrating principle that makes any family on mission work, as the name itself suggests. What's the mission? It's the same one God gave Adam and Eve, the same one Jesus gave the disciples—the purpose of a family on mission is to multiply the life of Jesus by reproducing ourselves into the lives of others, so they become disciples of Jesus who can then reproduce themselves into the lives of others.

In other words, the mission is Jesus. It is defined by Jesus, and it consists of Jesus. The life of Jesus is the organizing principle of every family on mission. Different families on mission have specific missional purposes toward certain neighborhoods or relational networks, of course (which we discuss below), but the mission is always multiplying the life of Jesus into that neighborhood or network. Our missional purpose is to reproduce Jesus by making disciples who make disciples.

MISSION IS
the integrating
principle that
makes any
family on
mission work.

As we discussed earlier, imitating Jesus means we...
- Listen for the **word of Jesus**
- Live into the **way of Jesus**
- Practice the **works of Jesus**

This forms our final little triangle within the big triangle of Family on Mission.

Let's discuss how we can lean into these generally, and then we'll share additional specific examples of how missional purpose looks in daily life.

LISTENING FOR THE WORD

Listening for the **word** of Jesus is an important part of imitating his life. Jesus told his disciples that the key to living a life in God's kingdom was letting his words abide in them. This means his words find a home in us. It means we meditate on his words. We listen for the word of Jesus in the Gospels and in prayer for guidance in our lives.

How do we live that out? We use the disciplines that followers of Jesus have used down through the centuries to listen for the word. It's actually not very complicated—we read our Bibles, and we pray with our family on mission. This is what we do every day. I read my Bible and let God speak to me through it every day, and every day I worship and pray with my *oikos*, and that keeps me abiding in the word of Jesus so that I'm always living in response to him.

YOU'RE CALLED to be a well and not a bucket.

And while it's great to come together for teaching, training, and encouragement, it's also important to remember that you're called to be a well, not a bucket. Eternal life is like a spring that bubbles up within you, and it's more important for you to uncover that well in your own life than it is for you to go and get filled up from someone else's well. This is how we abide in the vine that is Jesus. This is how we embrace and nurture the life of Jesus within us. As we do that, we become much more equipped to multiply that life into the life of others. You actually end up doing it without noticing it.

> ## IT'S IMPOSSIBLE
> **to be a disciple of Jesus if you don't know how to hear his word and respond.**

So this is what we train people to do if they want to be part of our family on mission. Part of your missional purpose needs to be training people to listen for the word of Jesus, so they can begin to live an interactive relationship with him. It's impossible to be a disciple of Jesus if you don't know how to hear his word and respond.

Oddly enough, that is pretty much what Sally and I do. We read our Bibles and pray every day, and just look for the next thing to do in response to Jesus' word. Before we knew it, there were people who wanted to hang around us. And eventually they wanted to learn how to do what we did, and before we knew it, we had an expanding covenant family with bigger and bigger missional purpose.

But it's all rooted in listening for the word of Jesus, every single day.

LIVING INTO THE WAY

In addition to listening for the word of Jesus, families on mission need to live into the **way of Jesus**. Often, this is the area that's easiest to skip. We know we're supposed to listen for the word of Jesus, and we want to be about the works of Jesus (which we'll talk about next), but we also must remember that Jesus had a way of doing things, and his way is not a random method or a incidental strategy. He was intentionally modeling methods and strategies for his disciples that he intended for them (and us) to imitate.

For example, the Western church has been trying to do discipleship through curriculum for years and years. We've come up with some of the best, most exciting, innovative, gorgeously designed discipleship curriculum ever seen in human history. And it's great stuff! But did Jesus do discipleship this way? No.

Moving Out in Missional Purpose | 87

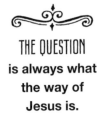

THE QUESTION
**is always what
the way of
Jesus is.**

He didn't do discipleship through information alone; he coupled it with access to his life so his disciples could imitate him. That's the **way** of Jesus. We live into that by giving others access to our life and offering ourselves as a living, breathing example to imitate.

Another example: lots of people have been trying to do discipleship one-on-one for years. But how did Jesus do discipleship? He hardly ever had a disciple one-on-one! He seemed to do a lot of evangelism one-on-one, but discipleship was a group thing, almost every time. He discipled people in groups so the learning could be multiplied.

When James and John get their mother to try to manipulate Jesus into giving them the best positions in his new kingdom, the rest of the disciples hear about it and are miffed! (I am inclined to think that at least the reason the other disciples were upset with James and John is that they didn't think of that idea first!) Jesus doesn't talk only with James and John about it, he gathers them all to talk about it, so they can all learn a lesson about leadership in the kingdom of God.[24]

Again, the question is always what the **way** of Jesus is. How did he do the thing we are trying to do as a family on mission? That's where we go for our inspiration and instruction. It's no mistake of history that the earliest followers of Jesus after the resurrection were simply called "The Way." As we read the Gospels and listen, the way of Jesus will become more and more apparent to us, and we'll know better how to lead our families on mission.

PRACTICING THE WORKS

Families on mission listen for the word of Jesus, we live into the way of Jesus, and finally, they need to be intentional about practicing the **works of Jesus**. This sometimes strikes us as a bit of a high bar, but Jesus was very clear about it when he told his disciples, "Whoever believes in me will do the works I have been doing."[25] If our families on mission are truly going to be

[24] Matthew 20:20-28
[25] John 14:12

a reflection and reproduction of the life of Jesus, we need to practice the works of Jesus, as uncomfortable as this may make us feel initially.

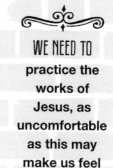

It's interesting to me that the first task the disciples are sent by Jesus to do is heal the sick, raise the dead, cleanse the lepers, and drive out demons. To us those things seem like a master class, but for Jesus, it was Discipleship 101. He gave them authority to heal before he gave them authority to teach.[26] Doing the works of Jesus has to be part of the discipleship process for our families on mission if we're going to take imitating Jesus seriously.

So we do that in our family on mission. We train people in the stuff that Jesus did. Every Sunday night at our *oikos* worship gathering, we pray for the sick, and very often people are healed. But it's not weird or out of control; it's just normal. We seek to be *naturally supernatural* as opposed to weirdly supernatural or merely natural. We don't hype it up or use King James English. It's all very normal, part of learning how to do the works of Jesus.

Again, taking our cues from Jesus, who never made a big theatrical production out of his healings, we simply come to our Father, assuming he wants good things for us, and we speak words of healing like Jesus did. It's loads of fun, because usually the kids are the very first people to ask for healing. They get prayed for but they also learn how to pray. Kids and adults together, praying for healing, every Sunday night. It's normal stuff for a spiritual family.

WHAT'S YOUR MISSIONAL PURPOSE?

Missional purpose is about listening for the word of Jesus, living in the way of Jesus, and practicing the works of Jesus. But that's a very "big picture" view of it. How does it translate practically into everyday life? How does a family on mission discover their own specific missional purpose? How do you find the people God is leading you to make disciples of?

[26] While he did tell them to proclaim the kingdom earlier, he didn't instruct them to make disciples and teach them until after the resurrection (Matthew 28:16-20).

It's important to define missional purpose and put language around because it affects how you make decisions about everything in your family on mission. Here's a really common example: should we let our son (let's call him Tommy) play on the soccer team? Well, it depends on whether that helps us live out our missional call or if it distracts us from it. Perhaps the families involved in soccer could be part of our missional purpose for a season, but perhaps we're already neck-deep in another missional context, and the soccer game schedule would mean we can't be as involved in our current missional context.

If we don't know why our family on mission exists, we have no framework for making those kinds of decisions. We may let Tommy play soccer because he really wants to, but later discover that it actually just made everyone tired and took us away from the place where God was actually beginning to do some work. We have to know why our family exists. Our missional purpose as a family is the integrating principle that allows us to move in the same direction together, and make wise decisions about what to do with our time and energy.

There are other resources we have, including workshops and books, which help families flesh this out in more detail, but for now, take a look at these example missional purpose statements from some of the families at 3DM.

JOINING JESUS IN HIS WORK

One family's missional purpose is stated this way: **Joining Jesus in his work.**

The phrase reflects the particular passions of this couple. One of the most important revelations God brought to them years ago was that salvation wasn't so much a matter of getting a ticket for heaven but was actually an invitation to be caught up in the ongoing work God was doing in the world. This has captivated them and moved them for many years, and so the concept of "joining Jesus" has found its way into their missional purpose as a family.

Their missional purpose is fairly broad, because it covers a wide range of activity, and will cover many years. For example, the father of this family travels quite a bit to train leaders at our Workshops and Learning Communities, but when he goes on a trip, he doesn't tell the kids that he "has to travel for work." He tells them that he is going to be joining Jesus in his work of training leaders in whatever city he is traveling to. The rest of the family prays for him and sends him out whenever he goes on a trip.

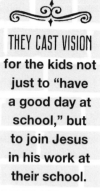

THEY CAST VISION for the kids not just to "have a good day at school," but to join Jesus in his work at their school.

The language of missional purpose makes a huge difference in how the children of this family experience his absence. They feel like they're part of what God is doing through a Learning Community that might be thousands of miles away. And they're right! They are part of it, because the language of their missional purpose invited them into it. They don't just think "Dad's gone." They know *why* he's traveling, because that's their family's purpose—joining Jesus in his work!

Another example is the way they talk around the breakfast table with their kids before they go to school. They cast vision for the kids not just to "have a good day at school" but also to join Jesus in his work at their school. The kids of this family go to school with the presupposition that their main job that day is to join Jesus in whatever he's up to in their school. They keep their eyes peeled for that, and then they report on the day around the dinner table, talking about what they saw God do, or what opportunities they feel they missed, and how it all went.

Things move in seasons, so during the summer when we don't have any Learning Communities, it allows them to focus more on joining Jesus in his work in the local community. Sometimes one of the kids' sports teams will be filled with people of peace, so they focus there for a while to see what God is up to, always seeking to join Jesus in his work. Whether it's a cross-country trip to train leaders or simply going to school or leading their Missional Community, this family is always **joining Jesus in his work**. That missional purpose is what helps the family keep moving forward as a pack in the same direction.

KNOW, SHOW, AND SHARE JESUS

Another family's missional purpose is defined by the phrase **Know, Show, and Share Jesus.**

This is the phrase they repeat often that animates their family's life. When they have people over from the *oikos*, they are seeking to know, show, and share Jesus. When they have people over from the neighborhood who don't know Jesus at all, they are seeking to know, show, and share Jesus. All of their family's activities are looked at through that lens, and it helps them make decisions about what to spend their time, money, and energy on. Will it allow them to know, show, and share Jesus? If not, they don't do it!

Again, having the language of missional purpose for explaining *why* a family is doing what they're doing helps tremendously in giving all the members of that family a sense of moving together in the same direction. It gives everyone a lens to evaluate whether or not to spend time, energy, or money on the opportunities in front of them.

BACK INTO THE HANDS OF ORDINARY PEOPLE

I'll give you one final example, our family on mission! 3DM and The Order of Mission function together, much like a family and a family business. Family is at the core of the organization that people see called 3DM. As a family on mission, then, we too have a missional purpose that drives everything we do and gives meaning to the various tasks we work on every day.

The missional purpose of 3DM is to change the world by changing America by changing the American church by **putting missional discipleship back into the hands of ordinary people**.

THERE ARE A LOT of mundane things that need to be done just to function together. But the same missional purpose animates it all.

This is the reason people move down to Pawleys Island to be part of the family: not because they want to hang out at the beach (we don't think), but because they want to be part of a family with this missional purpose.

This is what gives meaning to all the things that need to be done for us to function. Since 3DM employs quite a few people, a lot of mundane things need to be done for us to function together. But the same missional purpose animates it all. The person teaching at a workshop and the person looking over expense reports are part of the same family with the same missional purpose. It helps us make decisions about what to do, and gives meaning and significance to the tasks of each day.

GETTING STARTED

These are just a few examples of how missional purpose can be contextualized and specified based on how God has wired your family and the context he has you in. I encourage you to begin by first thinking about your **passions** as a family.[27] What kinds of things do you love to do? Do you love playing sports? Perhaps music? Do you love being outdoors? Do you enjoy being on the water? Do you absolutely love your neighborhood? Reading? Movies?

Then think about your **possessions**. I don't just mean the material things you own (but include those!), but all the various resources God has entrusted to you. Not just your financial capital but also your intellectual capital—perhaps you have an area of expertise that could be part of your missional purpose, like a counseling background or an ability to teach music or design websites. Also think about your physical capital—the time and energy you have available. Think about your relational capital—perhaps the people you know could be part of resourcing your missional purpose. Finally, and most importantly, think about your spiritual capital—perhaps there is wisdom you've gained over years of knowing God that you could bring into your missional purpose.

Finally, think about the **problems** you see around you. Think about your neighborhood or your workplace, the local school, or a park nearby. What are the needs you can see? Where are the areas of brokenness that you want to see God's kingdom break into? Where does God's will need to be done on earth as it is in heaven?

As you look at those three lists, begin to look for overlap and convergence. Is there a missional purpose making itself known to you? Don't worry if it isn't obvious right away. Sometimes it takes some time, discussion, and prayer to discern where God is giving you an opportunity to move out in mission.

---

[27] This is based on a tool Will Mancini taught us from his ministry Auxano (auxano.com).

10

∾ ENCOURAGEMENT ∾ FOR THE JOURNEY

STARTING OVER

Sally Writes:

We had been planning and talking about it for months. The international removal company had taken all our possessions and packed them into a container, and they were now sailing across the ocean on a ship aptly named *Faith*. Who knows when they would actually arrive? I had said a million goodbyes. The ones with my Mom and my sister were, of course, the hardest. But we were pressing on, looking forward, and not looking back.

We weren't looking back at the amazing ten years we had spent in Sheffield, building a team of wonderful, committed, and inspiring young adult leaders. We were choosing not to look back at our dear friends' faces as we set off that early misty morning of July 1, 2004. We sat in the car as the road snaked its way across the Pennine Mountains. I knew I was leaving behind all of my female relatives in one go—my mom, my sister, my nieces, my aunts, and my godmother. My two beautiful grown-up daughters were traveling with us this day but leaving in August to return to their college studies in the UK. I dreaded that tearful airport departure.

We had invited a large group of friends and followers to come with us on this new, unknown journey to Phoenix, and some of them were crazy and courageous enough to say yes. They were all coming and landing in the desert a few weeks later. In total there was a group of about fifteen of us, if

WE WERE A FAMILY,

not joined by genetics or bloodlines, but in purpose and passion.

you included children, bound together by a common mission and a set of values we held in our heart, and some vows we said before God. We were a family, not joined by genetics or bloodlines but in purpose and passion. At this moment, as we stepped onto the hot, dry tarmac at Phoenix Sky Harbor Airport, we were also bound as strangers in a foreign land.

We had no idea what would happen over the next ten years. We had no idea what battles would be fought, what scars and pain we would feel. We had no way of imagining what joys would inspire our souls or what depth of character in leadership we would learn. We didn't know what the future held, but we began by moving, one packing box at a time, into our new desert homes. We began by breathing in the hot air that burns your lungs and walking on the pavement that burns the soles of your feet.

We met and prayed together regularly. We worshiped and ate meals out of Crock-pots. We set long tables outside and barbecued shrimp and steak for Thanksgiving. We laughed over missing English foods and smells and shops. We loved the sunshine, the hot tubs, and the pools. We gathered others as we moved forward, some from the local church, some from the local community, and some from back in the UK. More children were added, and weddings took place, in deserted old pioneer chapels, and on freezing desert evenings. We were a family experiencing normal family traditions in unusual circumstances.

We held on, and on to each other, when, five years into the journey we were dealt a bitter blow. I can remember nights laying there praying and thinking, mentally circling the covered wagons that belonged to my "family" and checking everyone's spiritual, emotional, and physical health. All of this was harder and lonelier than I could ever have imagined, more tiring than I ever could have believed. But it was definitely what we were called to do. I stood on that. Mike stood on that. I built my faith and family on that rock. And the rock began to get bigger. By now, other people were also attaching their rocks of faith to ours. It was growing.

In late fall 2008, we were moving again. Sam, the fourteen-year-old son we had sent to high school knowing not one person, had graduated with honors and an experience of American life and culture that would be invaluable for him forever. He also graduated at the same time as a wonderful, intelligent, talented girlfriend who later became his wife. He had thrived in the desert, and his faith had grown strong and personal. He was now leaving to go on a yearlong internship with an international youth ministry. Our last child said goodbye.

Knowing this is what you spend years working to achieve, but fighting back the tears, we waved him through security at the airport. We took a deep breath, embarked on some intense spiritual battles, and moved across the country to the soft, moss-laden trees of South Carolina. Four families, four children. By now our middle daughter Libby had finished college, gotten married to a wonderful young man named Gavin, and was working for us part-time. She and Gavin also worked in a well-known traditional church in Charleston and volunteered as many hours as they could traveling up Highway 17 to help us out in Pawleys Island. We were a family on mission, on the move, setting up houses, businesses, and hopefully, changing for the better the small seaside community we lived in (and increasing Starbucks profits along the way).

We met every morning for worship and Word in a room no bigger than a closet. No one played a guitar so we just sang a cappella and followed the daily Scripture texts that the Moravians produce. It was a rhythm, a commitment. Some days a neighbor or friend would join us. They would learn about what we were doing, and how we were doing it, and would offer their skills. It was amazing and exhausting. We renovated our house just in time to host the first-ever 3DM Learning Community dinner, feeding fifty with Crock-pots bubbling and plastic glasses and plates ready. We kept the strong values of hospitality and accessibility that are important to us.

By now, five years further on, we have probably had more than five thousand people eat in our home and hundreds stay overnight. We have grown into a large team of about twenty-five in the local 3DM office, and about one hundred in the wider *oikos*. We do life together, we move as a pack, we are normal, and we are on a mission just like we wanted to be thirty-five years ago.

Never could we have imagined what those conversations spoken as teenagers, given over to

WE DO LIFE TOGETHER, we move as a pack, we are normal, and we are on a mission just like we wanted to be 35 years ago.

God, would do. Our family on mission now is a mixture of children who were either born into our family, married into our family, or attached themselves to us. They are young and old, married, single, divorced, remarried, separated, widowed—every type of person. Some work with us full-time, some work with us part-time, and some don't work with us officially at all. We come from many different backgrounds and cultures. But we are all committed to one thing: making disciples, and those disciples making disciples.

It's an honor and privilege for Mike and me to lead this group. We take it very seriously as the spiritual parents of this *oikos*. Every day we are reminded that it is messy, beautiful, complicated, hilarious, tiring, and life-giving. As this movement grows, we, too, grow and groan with it. We will still be doing this on the day we die. There is no retirement or vacation from this call. We know no other way.

Very occasionally, we look back and are amazed at what God has been able to do with that joyful, barefoot girl and that passionate young man, despite (and probably because of) our weaknesses. No wonder 2 Corinthians 12:9 has become a life verse for us, as Jesus says, "My grace is sufficient for you, for my power is made perfect in weakness."

JOIN US

We are meeting and relating to a growing group of people who are rising up as spiritual parents, putting in place predictable patterns, and moving out in missional purpose as families on mission. This is more than information in a book. It's a growing network of relationships, and we want you to be able to stay connected to others who are on this same journey.

Sign up for our email newsletter to stay connected to all of our upcoming Family on Mission training opportunities, like **workshops**, new **books** in this Family on Mission line, and **coaching** opportunities.

Also check out some of our new initiatives, like

- **Five Capitals** (for workplace Christians)
- **Launch** (for church planters)
- **Stand** (for women)
- **Wayfarer** (for youth/students)

Sign up at:

3dmovements.com/newsletter